PRAISE FOR THE WORKS C

SOME THING BLACK

"Waldrop's fine translation is a tribute to Roubaud's rich and often lyrical meditation on death . . . The poet exposes his psyche and the struggle he endures to make the language he uses in his craft transcend its inherent limitations. Fine reading."

—*Library Journal*

"Roubaud succeeds in creating an original, unforgettable poetic equivalent for that complex state of mind and feeling which arises in the presence of death."

—*Asylum*

THE GREAT FIRE OF LONDON

"How can any description do justice to this astonishing work? It is literally incomparable: I can think of no other book that suggests its scope, its methods, its effect."

—Harry Mathews

"Roubaud's book is remarkable . . . *The Great Fire of London* is an entirely sympathetic book to read, but in its careful organization it is also a heartening one, as showing the power of artifice to manage even the keenest of distress."

—*Times Literary Supplement*

"Roubaud is a humorous and sometimes earthy writer whose work can be enjoyed by a wide variety of readers."

—*San Diego Tribune*

OTHER WORKS BY JACQUES ROUBAUD
IN ENGLISH TRANSLATION

Our Beautiful Heroine
Some Thing Black
Hortense Is Abducted
The Great Fire of London
Hortense in Exile
The Princess Hoppy or, The Tale of Labrador
The Plurality of Worlds of Lewis
The Loop
Poetry, etcetera: Cleaning House

THE FORM OF A CITY
CHANGES FASTER, ALAS, THAN
THE HUMAN HEART

ONE HUNDRED FIFTY POEMS
(1991–1998)

JACQUES ROUBAUD

TRANSLATED BY KEITH AND ROSMARIE WALDROP

Dalkey Archive Press
Champaign and London

Acknowledgments:
Some of these translations have been printed in *Bombay Gin*, *Court Green*, *Golden Handcuffs*, *McSweeney's*, the *New Review*, *No: A Journal of the Arts*, *Walrus*, and the online magazines *Octopus* and *Drunken Boat*.

Rosmarie Waldrop would like to thank the Foundation for Contemporary Arts for a grant.

*Ouvrage publié avec le concours du
Ministère français chargé de la Culture – Centre National du Livre.*
[This Work has been published thanks to the
French Ministry of Culture – National Book Center.]

Partially funded by the University of Illinois at Urbana-Champaign
and by a grant from the Illinois Arts Council, a state agency

www.dalkeyarchive.com

Printed on permanent/durable acid-free paper and
bound in the United States of America

Contents

I
RERUNNING THE STREETS

INVENTORY

II
TWENTY SONNETS

SIX LITTLE LOGICAL PIECES

SQUARE DES BLANCS-MANTEAUX: MEDITATION ON DEATH

III
READING THE STREETS

HOMMAGE TO SÉBASTIEN BOTTIN'S TELEPHONE DIRECTORY

SONGS OF STREETS AND STREETS

QUIET DAYS AT PORTE D'ORLÉANS

UNDATED NIGHT, RUE SAINT-JACQUES

I

Rerunning the Streets
Inventory

Rerunning the Streets

Paris

after Raymond Queneau

The Paris we find to traipse
Is not the one we used to find
And we're not wild to get to
The Paris we will leave behind

Commentary on the Preceding Poem

J.R.:   Seven eight
seven eight
there me too I've got
a Verlaine
quatrain

R.Q.:   Well but yours
you copied

It's Taken

it's taken

from the Quai de Passy to the Rue Lacuée, from the Bois de Vincennes to the Avenue de l'Opéra, from 5 Rue Volta to the Quartier de l'Europe

it's taken

minutes days months years
springs summers winters falls

it's taken

from the Arc de Triomphe to the Rue de Prague, from (65) Boulevard de Sébastopol to Rue Abel, from the Place de la Bastille to Rue Férou

it's taken

umbrellas bumbershoots oilskins trench coats
caps and hats galoshes headgear

it's taken

from the Tuileries to the Rue Biscornet, from the Square de la Trinité to Rue Pierre-Leroux, from Carré Marigny to Avenue Daumesnil it's taken

taxis métros busses hearse and buggies
bateaux-mouches funiculars and
streetcars

it's taken

from Pont Mirabeau to Rue du Congo, from Belleville to Rue de
l'Abbé-Grégoire, from Boulevard Haussmann to Saint-Augustin

it's taken

shoes laces buttons belts
Mondays Tuesdays Wednesdays Thursdays
Fridays Saturdays Sundays and forever
Monday

from Rue de l'Oratoire to Rue de la Bienfaisance, from Rue de
Rivoli to Boulevard Malesherbes, from the BHV store to
the Impasse du Labrador
. . . .

it's taken

most of all, most of all
it sure has taken
rerunning the streets!

Rue Volta

No more "little old shop"
at 5 Rue Volta
"electric" relic
that progress swallowed whole

but in compensation
at the door of
the Vietnamese restaurant
at Nr. 7
the owner is arguing with
two rather prosperous
possible nationals
of the country that used to
be called Upper Volta
and I say to myself

"equatorial privations
life has compensated
sated sated on Rue Volta
sated gents from Upper Volta"

We Can No Longer Call on Saint Cloud

We can no longer call on *Saint Cloud* [i.e. Saint Nail]
when we see cars barreling down
those pedestrian crossings
supposed to "protect" us poor peripatetics
the white lines are no account
so flat
almost not there

we used to have good big traffic-nails
good nails with big shiny heads
heads so hemispheric
that *they* looked twice
before running you over
in between such nails

sometimes in August
(the dog days)
it'd get so hot they sank into the asphalt
got covered with tar
almost over their heads, just a tiny spot left
hardly big as a coin
or a ball [as in ball-bearings]
but you'd see them even so
like Tom Thumb's white pebbles
when you stepped off the curb of the boulevard
into the cacacar jungle

and when you crossed the street outside the nails
bearding the police
(who however haven't had beards
since time out of mind
(an expression moreover that's been out of use
a good long time))

when you crossed outside the nails
what daring!
what independence!
a gesture
almost
revolutionary!
Ah youth! Youth!
Ah!

but the nails are gone

perhaps there are some left
here or there
I was told of some in Rue de la Manutention
in the XVIth arrondissement
must make a pilgrimage
before they disappear

we could declare them monuments
I shall write to this effect
to the director of the Preservation Society

Boulevard de Clichy

Hell or Heaven, big deal!
But Nothing—
For Nothing itself to be gone!

Stamp-Collecting

At the Square Marigny not a single Raymond Queneau stamp.

Métro

In those days
The station *Assemblée-Nationale* was called *Chambre-des-Députés*
Line 1, *Vincennes-Neuilly*
Cluny station had not reopened
Since the end of the Occupation
Fantômas
Could have hidden a train there
We'd say "Getting off at the next?"
Preferably to misses and young ladies
Unaccompanied
By mother by husband by lover
On all the doors of all the cars was written
      Le train ne peut partir que les portes fermées
          Ne pas gêner leur fermeture
Thanks to which
The rules of French versification soon held no secrets for you
Ah Youth!
Youth!
Ah!

In those days
The steps of the stairs were of Carborundum
(Whose chemical
Formula you knew to be WC (W for
"Wolfram" (which is a pseudonym of "Tungsten"), and C,
For "Carbon"))
More indestructible than diamond
You gave up your seat for women pregnant to their hind teeth

Dyspeptic old men
And peroxide blondes
But not for veterans
Of either 1870 or 1914
Who in a rage would pull out their handicap card
Lift their pantleg above the ankle
Show their scars
And take the crowd to witness

And when the automatic gate
Shut in your face, at the time of the last Métro,
You went home on foot through the quiet streets
Past lamp posts, cats
And pigs on bicycles
Ah Youth!
Youth!
Ah!

In those days
Your ticket got punched and not only at Lilas
Were there first class cars
That smelled first class
Like Mireille Balin in *Pépé le Moko*
Before the train entered a station you read
On the tunnel wall
"Du Bo   du Bon   Dubonnet"
A reminder of before-the-war
For those who hadn't lived through it
(And those who had)
Pierre Dac
Sold anvils "on the run"
In the station *Campo-Formio*
Ah Youth!

Youth!
Ah!

But *in those days*
There was no station christened
BOBIGNY-PANTIN-RAYMOND QUENEAU
Right?
This
Makes up for
That

In Paris there are twenty arrondissements
There are also "three-or-four hundred lassies"
According to the song
If "three hundred" it's fifteen per arrondissement
If "four hundred" they average twenty
In any case not many
And I have never seen them "dance among the grassies."

The twenty arrondissements of Paris are numbered
Nr. 1 is called the Ist Arrondissement
Nr. 2 is called the IInd,
And so on (up to twenty).

In the Ist arrondissement is the main post office in Rue du Louvre. You can mail your letters there; even on Sunday. That is very convenient.

The IInd arrondissement is remarkable because it houses (and will at least till 1998) the Bibliothéque Nationale.

In the IIIrd arrondissement you will find "the verdant Square des Arts et des Métiers." A character in the novel *Les copains* by Mr. Farigoule (alias Jules Romain) announces that he is about to go there "on the gadget that accelerates the feet."

The IVth arrondissement is known for the BHV department store.

The Vth for its Panthéon, "a jewel of Gothic art."

Of the VIth we'll remember the Luxembourg Gardens and its statues. Raymond Queneau has drawn up a quasi exhaustive list of them in *Courir les rues* (a book of poems by that author).

The VIIth is towered over by the Eiffel Tower.

The VIIIth by the Arc de Triomphe.

In the IXth is the present residence of M. Roubaud who is composing the present prose poem.

The Xth arrondissement is cut through by the canal Saint-Martin where once was the Hotel du Nord whose famous "atmosphere" we know. Is it also here that Louis Jouvet made, to my mind no less famously, this definitive statement: *"Les mères de famille vous disent 'mère . . . de famille.'"*

The XIth arrondissement is not the location of the CHU Saint-Antoine Hospital where Georges Perec worked.

This CHU is in the XIIth (unless I'm mistaken; in which case it's *vice versa* or *Lycée de Versailles* as Pierre Dac used to say (unless it was Francis Blanche)).

In the XIIIth I'll point out the Park Montsouris and its Eastern boundary, the Rue Gazan where François Caradec of the Oulipo lives.

The XIVth has the street of la Tombe-Issoire, but not the street of la Folie-Méricourt (which is in the XIth).

The XVth is far, very far. In its Rue des Favorites is the Center for Postal Money Orders.

The XVIth arrondissement has Pomp. Rue de la.

Entering the XVIIth one thinks of Aristide Bruant and his song (I quote from memory, poorly) *"La morale de cette histoir'là /d'cette histoir'là / c'est que les filles qu'a pas d'papa / qu'a pas d'papa 'faut pas les envoyer à l'école / aux Batignolles."*

The XVIIIth is the Butte.

The XIXth is feeling for nature (at the Buttes-Chaumont, obviously).

And now we finally get to the XXth arrondissement. We go to the Mur des Fédérés (not many visitors).

The entire surface of Paris is parceled out among the twenty arrondissements. Not an inch escapes them.

Each arrondissement of Paris is a compact space. One can walk continuously from one point of an arrondissement to another without ever leaving it.

Certain pairs of arrondissements share a border: the Ist borders the IInd, the IInd borders the IIIrd, etc.

Whenever one crosses the border of one arrondissement to go into another one always feels a little thrill: thus M. Roubaud whenever he crosses the Rue d'Amsterdam where he lives. Because the side with uneven numbers is in the VIIIth, and not in the IXth (which the post office will take upon itself to remind you of by stamping a letter addressed to M. Roubaud in the VIIIth with a severe "wrong address, letter delayed"). But where exactly is the border? Is it a narrow band that runs the whole length of the street?

The most remarkable spots of Paris are those where several arrondissements meet: thus on Place de l'Etoile the VIIIth, XVIth and XVIIth. The crossroad of Boulevard de Belleville, Rue de Belleville, Rue du Faubourg-du-Temple and the Boulevard de la Villette belongs by right to four arrondissements: the Xth, XIth, XIXth and XXth. There are other examples that you can make your own list of.

Four and no more than four colors are sufficient to color the map of Paris in such a way that no two adjacent arrondissements are of the same color.

Between the XVth and the XVIth, under the Pont Mirabeau, flows the Seine.

Queneau in November

I see him walk along the Seine
Color of sky color of water
He's dreaming of a world well dreamed
Where numbers tend to give in better
To machinations of the poem
I can see how the leaves are fallen
In puddles of low fading light
Is it December? or November?

And as soon as the leaves have fallen
One takes one's notebook out for poems
Walking the bank along the Seine
It's evening now: the poor sunlight
Is getting weaker. He'd do better
To let his shadow take to water
Under the showers of November
Dreaming meanwhile the number dreamed

Shadows in fall soak up the water
Our pumps don't do it any better
Gummed up with all those dead leaves fallen
Into the gutters of November
The evening now directs its light
To the tablet reserved for poems
Where is inscribed the number dreamed
While walking here along the Seine

Here exigencies of the poem
Can be read in the clearest light
So must it all fall in the water
The whole scaffolding he has dreamed
For his octogrammic November?
Alas it could have been far better
In April. All along the Seine
The leaves of all the trees have fallen

Alas it would have been far better
In April rather than November
Shorter would have been the poem
Pleasant the banks along the Seine
In April. Month so often dreamed
So clear the sky, fountain of light
Up fly the leaves already fallen
Back to the trees down by the water

O puddles of so sad a light!
Nevertheless, the number dreamed
Four by four who could do better
So many images have fallen:
Oyez, ahoy, rudds of the Seine
Oy, good oysters of November
Night's negative ignites the water
Plenty material for a poem

Was it December or November
I see him walk along the Seine
Holding his page up to the light
Blackened with figures, damped with water
He walks upon leaves that have fallen

He's dreaming now of the world dreamed
Where words and numbers in the poem
Take to each other, blending better

I write here once more the word "dreamed"
I write the words here: "number," "water"
I ask myself: well why November?
Why on earth oyster, and why poem?
The leaves have all already fallen
Along the sad banks of the Seine
It's raining now. For trees that's better
Even and gradual the light.

Envoi

Fall of a dream in some November
I've watered this pome in the Seine
The best I'm able, by my light.

Inventory

The Gioconda

To see Mona
Lisa, real fans don't trot
off to the world's end, no not
even to the Louvre

They go where Rue de
La Rochefoucauld crosses Rue
Notre-
Dame-de-Lorette, they
step into the café
and there she is

The painting's on the wall
in beige and cream
the frame beige-cream plus a touch of orange
the canvas signed
in the artist's own hand
E.
Mérou.
It's Mona all right
the Mona Lisa of Mérou.

Emile Mérou? Eugene Mérou? Ernest Mérou?
could be Emily, Eugenia, Ernestine?
who knows?

Behind her well washed glass
Mona Lisa looks content

she looks at me
she smiles
without the littlest condescent
without an atom of mystery
all placid
calm
a beauty

Well whatchexpect?—it's Mona Lisa!

Real fans don't trot off to
world's-end or
the Select-Bar at the Rotonde
or deep into the jungle nor
to the islands of the Sonde
nor to Peru
but from the Sacré Coeur it's just a few
steps, Mona Lisa's on view

Mona Lisa, Lisa Mona,
Mona Lisa by Mérou

So
let's give a-one and a-two
for Lisa, the
MonamonalisabyMérou!

Sacré–Coeur!

Sacré-Coeur!
O I see you
Babybottle
with your big tit in the shape of the cross

Sacré-Coeur!
but you're seven babybottles!
I see you all perfectly from down the hill
in Square Saint-Pierre
three little babybottles
three medium babybottles
and one big fat one

It's evening
the glorious sky scoots over
so the angels can come and suck at
three little babybottles
three middling babybottles

But you
big babybottle
you are for Baby Jesus
ah!
may he not bruise his lips
on your cross-shaped tit

27

Informal Intimate Ode to the Copy
of the Standard Meter in the Rue de Vaugirard

Under the arcades in Rue de Vaugirard, between Rue Garancière
and Rue Férou, one reads

STANDARD METER

The National Convention, in order to encourage use of the metric
system, had sixteen standard meters (in marble) placed in the busiest
spots of Paris.
The meters were installed between February 1796 and December
1797. This is one of the last 2 in Paris and the only one still in its
original place.

time has passed, old friend
since we first met
I was twelve and you
one hundred forty-eight
it was winter
nineteen hundred forty-four
it was cold
the fountains in the Luxembourg were frozen
the statue population
shivering
asses of the lady statues
all white with white
frost on
white marble (where it wasn't green)
and so cold

I stretched out on the ground
to be parallel to you

to measure myself
against an exact measure
much more conclusive than the tapes
or metersticks
or strings
my father used
to check how my
brothers my sister and I
were growing
if not visible to the eye
visible at least by lines penciled
month after month
on the kitchen door frame

I trusted you
I trusted the Convention
that had placed you
and your fifteen siblings
at various spots in Paris
so that citizens would get used
to contemplating
the ten-millionth part
of a quarter of the earth's meridian
I never believed in the platinum-iridium prototype
in some building in Breteuil
even less the absurd story
of wavelength
but I believed in you

now I'm old
I've grown stopped growing begun to ungrow
and that's only the beginning before it all ends
with a notable absence of *all* measurement

but you
I'd say you haven't changed
you haven't budged
an inch
if I dare use this term
barely some expansion and contraction
from unavoidable heat-and-cold
because of nights days seasons
for me you've stayed the same
dignified, thin, tense, straight, calibrated in
    decimeters, between your two tips topped by
    your family name, METER, by your Convention
    hat, impassive,
horizontal

spring nineteen
hundred ninety-
four I'm here to visit you
as from time to time
when I happen to be in the area
you won't mind if
I don't lie on the ground this time
at your feet which aren't feet
people in the street might find it bizarre
for a gentleman of my age
even in front of the Luxembourg Palace
where the senators
of the Fifth Republic doze
this might seem
an ill-measured action

Rue Duguay-Trouin

Getting off the 56 bus I turned left, then again left at the first corner, into Rue Duguay-Trouin.

At the end of the street, Rue Huysmans went off left at an angle.

But to the right, again at an angle, there was still Rue Duguay-Trouin!

The end of this end of the street was not the end of the street, Rue Duguay-Trouin.

The Rue Duguay-Trouin made a turn to the right and elbowed back to Rue d'Assas

Whence it had come.

The first days of nineteen hundred forty-five.

I had gotten off the 56 at Rue d'Assas and discovered the secret of Rue Duguay-Trouin

Which branches off from Rue d'Assas and then goes back to it.

O wonder!

Marvel!

O unfathomable mystery of the great city!

I walked several times the triangle two sides of which are filled by Rue Duguay-Trouin.

Today, December 31, 1993, at three o'clock in the afternoon, it's raining in Rue d'Assas, at the 56 stop.

It's raining in Rue Duguay-Trouin

Which is empty.

And I'm amazed.

What amazes me today is not that Rue Duguay-Trouin still returns to Rue d'Assas after a rather short side-step,

But that I remember so vividly, after forty-nine years, my amazement at this very Parisian phenomenon of street planning.

My amazement is all I remember.
Yet it was nothing worth making all this fuss about
Back then
Or even less today.
But we must gather our amazements where we may.
Especially on a 31st of December.

A Hotel in Rue Notre-Dame-de-Lorette

A thousand times and more going down this street
I made the effort
not to see it
but in vain

Sure of having passed it
I'd lift my eyes
and there it was
and every day, for a moment, I'd nurse the crazy hope
that overnight the mistake had been corrected,
but no
it was still

MODIAL HOTEL

As anticipated
by the natural pessimism
of my orthographic subconscious.

Walking back up the street
in the evening
I'd've become used to it
wasn't shocked any more
but the relief was temporary
did not outlast the night and there again
in the morning I'd look
with the same ocular indignation

Now the MODIAL HOTEL has been remodeled
It has changed its name its color
and no doubt its rating
now it's called
MODIAL HOTEL EUROPE
a name so
banal that it no longer causes any confusion in my mind.

The Champs-Élysées Roundabout

There are not many still around who sum up torpid
souls
"in a few round smoke rings"
"that perish in further rings"
(. . . et, I presume, cetera)
it's a while since I've encountered in my reading
roundels or Roundheads or even roundhouses
and without the *Petit Robert* dictionary I couldn't tell you
the meaning of *ronde-bosse* [i.e., figure in the round]
which is an architectural term
first used in the sixteenth century; but
in the softcore porn of the fifties
(the *série blonde*)
it meant what we ordinarily called
roberts, boobs
(big or little)
("you could see her boobs: what knockers")
(that's Sartre)
(more recently we were saying: *roploplo*
as you can read
on a column at the streetcar station
Porte-de-l'Hôpital in Strasbourg)
still, according to the *Robert* (*petit*), *ronds-de-cuir*, for quill-pushers
on their round stools, is hardly more than a hundred years
old and already
obsolete

good thing we still have the
Roundabout
said I to myself, crossing the Champs-Élysées.

Pont des Arts

I happen to be walking
across the pont des Arts
a bridge under which flows
"the wave" (of
the Seine) "so
fed up with
eternal gawking"

it's also flowing
under pont
Sully and pont Neuf and
isn't it rather—
under pont Mirabeau—that
the Seine's fed-up-ness
is from its "under the-bridge-of-our-
arms going"?

no doubt
but I can't see why
it wouldn't be fed up
a few bridges upstream

I sit on a bench be-
tween bushes
recently planted on
the bridge
see ahead of me
the Eiffel Tower

and the wind? there's no
wind

A Poem for Claude Roy

For more than twenty years
I've sometimes, I've often
during the year, from there or here
walked diagonally across
the Place Dauphine and the old bridge
over the left arm of the Seine
where the river pulse beats
at the feet of the Vert-Galant

for more than twenty years
I've sometimes, I've often
entered the courtyard of #16
of the street to chez
Claude
Roy

I climb up three flights I mount and count
the 28 steps to the first floor
the 25 steps to the second
the 23 steps to the third
(the count I'm pleased to note
comes out the same as always)
as 3 plus 5 is 8
(generally)
we have here (once we subtract 20)
the reverse of the beginning
of a Fibonacci series

the series that secretly moves toward the golden number
as everyone knows

I enter

at Claude's place there is always a cat
(sometimes it's a tom)
"a cat moving among the books"
and some "all-weather friends"
without whom he couldn't live
(I'm not forgetting
Loleh)

we talk

we talk about books
and again books
books on this and that and that again
books that we've read, reread, could read, couldn't
      read, could still read
that I should've read
should read
because there are many books
I've not read
that he has and
that I should read
he's right
(it's true he had
a head start
and is no turtle when it comes to reading
but I'm neither hare nor Achilles
and even if I were I couldn't catch up
as was once shown by Mister Zeno

"Zeno, cruel Zeno," zealous demon!)

but back to the books
we talk of
some are good
some less good some not good
but luckily some
are marvelous
there are
marvelous books of poetry
and at some moment or other we get around to
    talking
about poetry
that is, we talk
about time

about poetry
"at the edge of time
the full summer night   where the road was white"
and it's then I hear
these words of poetry from summer nineteen hundred
    eighty-two
when time for him had almost decided to stop
to stop
the poetry
the voice of poetry in the conversation of mankind

he said
"Who will wake up at the end of my dream?"
he said
"In back of the shadow there is a song"
or
"The clock's pendulum in winter"

that's how poems began in those days
though a poem begun might never get finished
you couldn't know
of all the poems dashed onto the page
would one, on turning, end up in the black?

"Came a garden tonight / It had no address"
said the poem
"Silent words that the flakes / Write on stubble and
    plough"
said the poem
"This serious pin-point way / Specific to the mammal
    heart"
said the poem
"The little garden spider / between two rosebush
    stems"
the poem said

poetry
odor of time
"Odor as of apples shaken down by the wind"

poetry
that we read and will read and will cite and recite and
    talk about
as long as "the wellspring of time"
still counts "the days."

envoi (January 1998)

poetry
that we've read and spoke and spoke of

as long as the wellspring of time
still counted the days

Poem of the Eiffel Tower

Eiffel Tower! I came to see
and I see
but to see what one sees is not that easy
in words that have but half a dozen referents
at best
what I could say I see has no bearing
before what I see and haven't said
and won't say not knowing how to say
what by the way I cannot show either
Eiffel Tower! I don't see you
you that I came to see in order to talk about this seeing
in the framework of my poetry campaign
I consider this part of my duty
as a poet
it would indeed be difficult
to talk of Paris without talking of the tower
even Apollinaire. . .
however I don't think Réda pays much attention to it
in *Les ruines de Paris*
nor Queneau in *Courir les rues*
perhaps they find it too obvious
or
they have seen it so much that they don't see it any more
in any case
they abstain from comment
but Apollinaire, I remember
addresses it as a shepherdess
(just before addressing it, "O")

if a shepherdess these days she'd have on her hands
not so much bridges but
those curious sheep
inane young women and men who invade the space
    between her feet
and take up the whole esplanade
preparing to bleat
in honor of a pope's visit
who is certainly not the most sympathetic of the popes
who've succeeded one another at the head of Peter's church
(if you'll permit an agnostic to pass such a judgment)

I've perhaps not chosen the best moment
for an Eiffel Tower poem

Boulevard Pereire

between Boulevard Pereire
north side
and Boulevard Pereire
south side
bowers
bulging with red
roses and pink
roses and
white roses
rain down petals wet
with the rain of a Pentecost Monday in June

if I were fifty years younger
they would come down tongues like as of
fire—I would understand all dialects
and would speak to the roses
red roses, pink roses, white roses
in the original tongue.

Rue Étienne-Jodelle

Rue Étienne-Jodelle
starts at the villa Pierre-Ginier near Rue Hégésippe-Moreau
short
and remarkably uninteresting
a gust of wind blows an "angel hair" across my cheek
it comes from nearby Montmartre cemetery
(I can see its wall in Rue Ganneron)
cemeteries nourish dandelions
so that the dead can, according
to a time-honored
expression, contemplate their roots
the umbel of the dandelion is like a feathery
head
before the wind scatters it in the air
Shakespeare compares it to the broom of little chimney sweeps
a mysterious comparison
that leaves commentators perplexed
"golden boys and girls all must / like chimney sweepers come to dust"
dust! everything is and will be dust!
"oh golden boys
and girls"
you too!

a couple steps farther a house where Cézanne worked called
now *villa des Arts*

well I'll go as far as Avenue de Clichy
and it won't be "the end, harbor, daybreak"

The Days Grow Shorter

The days grow shorter
not so long ago
they were long
and not so long from now
they'll be short

At this moment they are not very long
but also, not very short
it's all a question
of how you measure

But how do we know
these days were long
or that those
will be short?
we can't put them side by side
to compare

To measure them
we use space
the space of a clock
the space of a sun dial
the space of an hour glass

And there we see
the days grow shorter
no doubt about it

They're also paler
more sullen
damp
sad

But perhaps
it's not that days grow shorter
perhaps it's just that our
timespan's elastic

On the other hand we have to admit that every
day, if there is less day
there is more night
we get a bit less day
we get a bit more night
the sum remains constant

Basically
complain as we may
we've always compensation.

The Days Grow Longer

Days grow longer
The days are children of a big family
their father the Sun
every morning
sticks them at the foot of an oak, heels together
spinal column very straight
belly, eyes and chin pulled in,
in the evening
at the moment of dusk
the precise moment when the red disc bites the horizon
he claps
his big fatherly hand on their heads
and notes
by notching the oak bark
the progress
of their growth

But maybe there is actually only one single day
always the same
a single day identical to itself
in its innermost being
an only son
who's growing
while his sister the night
dwindles

If this is so why do we say "the days"?
how can we say days
are growing?

In Spring

Approximate spring
(21 March + or - x days
(x variable—if x approaches 365 we say
"ain't no more seasons!"
or we say
"lousy spring!"))

approximate spring, I said
the trees
no longer dressed
only in sparrows
leaves
are coming back to the trees
or else the trees
are picking up leaves
they're turning green

for some time we saw them
hesitate, finger the air,
scrutinize the clouds
watch their neighbors out of the corner of an eye
then suddenly there they go
they take the plunge

approximate spring
(it's the ones with "caducous" leaves that go for it
the English call them *deciduous*
because of their decisiveness
"persistent leaved" evergreens with

nothing left to decide
pull a long face
dirt-coated
from years of urban
soot)

on the trees
baby leaves shiver
little leaves feel their way, fragile, slowly
unfolding their buds
the breeze   holds them   tenderly   on their stems
as saith the po-wet

yes!
the leaves go for it, proliferate
profusely
trees spread, mirror themselves in fountains
windows
puddles
the blue of the sky
that's it
spring's here

so it happened
this year (nineteen hundred ninety-four)
in Paris
in the Tuileries
in the Luxembourg Gardens
in Park Montsouris
in the Square des Blancs-Manteaux
at the foot of Sacré-Coeur in the Square Saint-Pierre
I checked

and have no reason to think
it was otherwise
elsewhere

A Couple in Unison

Rue Rambuteau
Sunday
at eleven

he and she
she and he
in unison

dip their heels in the gutter
that drains
the fish store slush

then
carefully
scrape them
against the sharp edge of the sidewalk

having tread some ripe shit

whatcha know
I say to myself
here's a couple in real unison

alas!
not the case—the one and the other
off on their separate shitty way

Mother and Daughter

"You can go pee outside, at the corner
not in the café, it's too dirty."
"And stop that yammering
or home you go."

The girl has pigtails and a blue flowered dress
the mother blond chignon over sour puss

after that
they go over to McDonald's

in my family
we said
"yammying."

Seen.
Heard.

Noted.

Autumn in Rue du Printemps

The foliage on Boulevard Pereire (looking south)
Is already turning
Red

Shocking.
They should block off that resolute-
Ly drab street from Spring Street with
A big tick curtain and not draw it
Until spring.

Square Louis-XVI

I take advantage of a shady bench on Square Louis-XVI. But I turn my back (either you're republican or you're not) on the "atonement chapel ("monument built and consecrated by King Louis XVIII") where the King and Queen Marie-Antoinette rested for twenty-one years (some siesta) before being taken to the royal sepulchre in Saint-Denis." There is a big "Oriental plane tree" on either side of the façade. In front of me, a bed of white roses; I don't see any lilies. Not a single "grand proud lily sways in the wind." Perhaps it's not the season for lilies. And in any case there is no wind.

At the third floor of the building on my left on Rue Pasquier, a surface technician with green vest and black face is cleaning a large window. The building on my right proudly sports (when one sports it's always, as far as I know, proudly) five vertical bas-reliefs (*sculpt. G. Saupicque*): from left to right a camel, an elephant, a crocodile, a shark and a tiger. These jungle beasts are at third floor level. Five tropical and fabled birds that I cannot identify nest under the ledge of the fifth. This building, which does not bear a date, belongs to the Bayerische Bank. It forms the corner of Rue Pasquier and Rue des Mathurins.

The back of the chapel must be known in the neighborhood as a place to piss in case of need (an "*emergency-pissoir*" you might say). Already three times some guy walked in front of me in that direction and reappeared a few moments later adjusting his pants in a manner that leaves little doubt. At nine o'clock in the morning on a 13th of August at the end of the twentieth century I could hardly suppose a secret pick-up for debauchery (an anachronistic, nostalgia-satisfying "cruising station") and/or resurgent monarchism. Perhaps it's simply that there's an honest, perfectly legitimate but modest convenience tucked away in the shrubbery. This hypothesis however seems highly unlikely. I do not check. I walk away.

Our Kings

Prévert made fun of the kings of France, who could not count to twenty. The Paris city fathers, it seems, know only three of them: Louis XVI who has his square; Louis-Philippe who has an arcade and a bridge, but no number (kings have a first name and a number, which together form a mineralogical label for their carriage); and Saint Louis, the best off, with a courtyard, another bridge, and an "-en-l'isle" (which is very "old France").

When I think how Maurice Chevalier sang: "The cavalry with their Louis XV legs," they could have given him a street among the antique dealers around Saint-Antoine.

There is nothing, but nothing, for the others: neither for the Pious (who is at the same time the Debonnaire), nor for the sluggard Stammerer; nothing for d'Outremer nor for Sluggard number two; nothing for the Fat, the Young, the Lion, the Quarreler, the Well-Beloved . . . What negligence!

Rue Tronson-du-Coudray

At the corner of the street named for Tronson-du-Coudray (1750-1798), defense counsel for Marie-Antoinette, is the restaurant *A. G. the Poet*. A. G. (Antoine Gayet) offers us his *Marine Poem* (served only in the evening).

Tronson du Coudray. I find this name, with its suggestion of cutting and sewing, provocative. Seeing on the streetsign his date of death, 1798, I hope for a moment that the Thermidorians of the Directory repaired the omission of their Montagne colleagues and did not resist the pleasure of unsewing his head with a cut of the guillotine.

(But no. As I learn a little later in the *Robert of Proper Names*, Guillaume died in exile in Guyana. Pity: a fine occasion was missed for a bit of Cratylism, approximate and after the fact.)

Square Gabriel-Pierné

The old fountain in the Carmes Market
designed in 1830 by Alexandre Évariste Fragonard
a Janus figure with commerce on one side and on the other
abundance
the head, crowned with a tutti-frutti hat
(like Carmen Miranda (in a Busby Berkeley film)
who was much appreciated by Ludwig Wittgenstein),
spouts water from two metal mouths
into a round basin twenty centimeters deep and at most one meter
    in diameter
a plastic plaque indicates, by icon, that the water is not drinkable:
faucet   glass under it, crossed out
but there's another, more surprising image,
a swimmer doing the crawl among green stylized waves,
forbids also bathing

bathing?
I'm flabbergasted

Place Paul-Verlaine

"The black-currant river flows unwatched
In strange haphazard ways"
"The shadows of trees in the river fog
Vanish like smoke"

Well.
The only black-currant river here is the soda trickling over a little
    girl's hand
In front of the swimming pool at Butte-aux-Cailles.
There are three of them crossing before the vertical blue neon of
    the Hotel Verlaine
The biggest walks reading a comic strip
Perhaps a new episode of *Babar:*
"Paul and that rascal Arthur"

Verlaine and Rimbaud each have a "villa"
But that's by Métro Danube:
Two dead-ends.

Rue de la Colonie

Rue de la Colonie
Runs parallel
To Rue de la Providence

And each of the two
(If one is, the other is also, right?)
Perpendicular
To Rue Bobillot
"Sergeant of the Engineer Corps
Dead in Tonking
(1860-1885)"

At number 76b a
DOGGIE CENTER

Rue Jonas

Rue Jonas
"Biblical figure"
Crosses Rue Samson
In the middle of which flourishes a small garden
of dahlias
(named after Dahl, Danish botanist)
"Dahli-a, dahli-a
Loved by Deli-lah"
*(Max
Jacob)*
I said to myself
Walking along there

*(There is a Rue Max-Jacob near Rue Poterne-des-Peupliers
But no Rue Dahl no-
Where)*

November

You'd only catch an allergy
if you tried too hard to face
the Arc de Triomphe on the Place
de Coudenhove-Kalergi

We are alone, me and a cat
come to piss below the plaque
of this Austrian diplomat

(Advocate of European unity, founder of the
Council of Europe 1894-1972)

November! For what retreat could we go pack!

XVth *Arrondissement*

no doubt in possession
of a smattering of Latin
an old man in Rue de la
Croix-Nivert smirks
before a store window
of *lingerie féminine*
"IN FINE"

XVth Arrondissement, 2

Rue Desnouettes
a pair of streetcar tracks
come out from under a gate
cross the street
and disappear under another
gate

Boulevard Arago

Boulevard Arago
Under the chestnut trees
A urinal
The last perhaps
Of the old kind

Against the wall
Of the Santé
Which won't be the last prison.

Autumn in the Air

A little coolness at the corner of summer's lips
Soon there'll be
"Autumn in the air"

History

Rue de Saint-Pétersbourg
has regained its name from
before the Second-World-War
when it was besieged by
an army of unknown nationality
under a name not to be mentioned
during the battle of Tsaritsyne

Charles Martel

Charles Martel was a naval officer
born 1867
died 1924
after having vanquished the Arabs at Poitiers in 732

if you don't believe me
go to Rue Dulong
and you'll see

he is entitled to an alley, the
alley of Commandant-Charles-Martel
that runs into Rue de Rome

on Rue Dulong
there is a Korean restaurant
called
Land of Tranquil Morning

astounding, no?

Few Memories

I have few memories of Métro Exelmans
I have few memories of Métro Buzenval
I have few memories of Métro Marx-Dormoy
I have few memories of Métro Corvisart

I have few memories of Métro Corentin
Cariou   I have few memories of Métro Co-
Rentin-Celton   I have few memories of Mé-
Tros Alexandre-Dumas and Saint-Fargeau. And

Of Javel-André-Citroën I have hardly
Any nor yet of Malakoff-Étienne Do-
Let.
    — Few?
            — Few.
                — Hardly any?
                    — Hardly. I have few, very few

Memories of Métro station Philippe-Auguste,
You see. And to top it all I really have ab-
Solutely no memory of Métro Croix-Rouge

                — That does not surprise me
        This Métro station was shut down during the war
                And never reopened

Avenue Ernest-Reyer (Parkside)

A turning sprinkler waters the lawn green with green grass and with each turn of its swivel goes beyond the grass to water the walk all the way up to the blue-green bench where I've sat down to watch the turning sprinkler water the green grass of the green lawn the grass individually each element distinct and the green lawn as a whole which makes two very different greens I sit here feeling the cool of the water that laps and then evaporates from the dust at my feet where three sparrows have come to bathe in the dust still moist with the coolness of the turning sprinkler in this park at the southern extreme of the XIVth Arrondissement between the Avenue Ernest-Reyer and the "Périf" or Boulevard Périphérique the grass exudes its sweat of water and sun the turning sun also sprinkles the walk and the lawn it also turns but more slowly and when I look up from my notebook it has reached me it's drenching my feet and the turning fountain has also moved a bit it now splashes the sides of the blue-green bench on my left I no longer feel the breath the breeze of the spray of water of its coolness the sun now beats on my shoulder it tells me get up and go

Rue Guillaume-Tell

"After the reign of anorexic stars
Glamor goddesses now reclaim the market."
So *Glory* fills me in. By dint of sem-
Piternal walking I'll become poetic.
In William-Tell-Street I search vainly, and
For no good reason, for love-apples. In Ed-
L'Épicier's discount store are apple-apples,
But no arrows for Tell's epic athletic
Gesture to be mimicked in situ (well,
Onomastically). Rain threads distorting
Mirrors in sidewalk cracks. 10 Rue Galvani
Is Claude Berge's address—he of the Ouli-
Po. I pass in K-Way, cap (no béret).
The direction of Porte de Champerret.

Kitty O'Shea

now that I'm learning to drink
in preparation for my approaching
retirement

sometimes
in the afternoon
I go to the Kitty O'Shea
I order
"a pint of Guinness, please"

I sit down with a book
in English
and stay an hour
by myself
drinking and reading slowly
sip by sip
the bitter and cool pitch black

the Kitty O'Shea is a renowned Irish pub
in the heart of Paris
a few steps from the Tuileries
nevertheless
I imagine I'm in London
a way as good as another
not to be in this city
where I live

A Good Day

Today was a good day
Three times I was asked directions
1. A Japanese couple was looking for the Opera
On avenue de l'Opéra
2. A man from the provinces was looking for the church Notre-
Dame-des Victoires on
Place Notre-Dame-des-Victoires
3. A young woman was looking for the Rue du Général-Delestraint
Right at the exit of Métro Porte-de-Saint-Cloud
Really, it was a good day

Hermit

Rare
Pleasure

To post
A letter at the
Main Post
Office (Louvre)
On a 15th of August

But to whom?

Impasse de Nevers

né, nay, nay, nell, nay, né on, neon, nor on,
need, neo, new, n'you, knee you, nu, nuance, nuke,
navy, navel, no well, no, no, no way, now, now,
no, nay, nay, nudge, nude, nub, nubile, numb, neume
not may, not my, mai, may, moo, menial, nil,
nemial, nay may, nave, name, no aim, noon, nose,
nosegay, nude, neu, neuter, nog, noggin,
nous, new, mew, mew, meeow, minion, minime, nimbus,
nimble, nimmer, ni meurt, number, nummer, mummer,
moon, no on, noon, no, nay, nouveau, nova,
n'eve, ne, nev, neve, never, never

Dream of February 11, 19—

I'm in a café; a café in Paris, like the one near the Métro Liège where I go every morning to read the paper and have breakfast. It is morning (a young blond woman is moving a wet mop between the tables, under the customers' feet, under mine) but it is still dark. I spread the paper in front of me; the owner comes and puts an "au lait" on the table and two slices of bread and butter; he takes the two ten franc coins that I fish out of my pocket and gives me one franc eighty change. Somebody comes in.

Dream of August 17, 19—

I'm in a café; a café in Paris, like the one near the Métro Liège where I go every morning to read the paper and have breakfast. It is morning (a young blond woman is moving a wet mop between the tables, under the customers' feet, under mine) but it is not dark. I spread the paper in front of me; the owner comes and puts an "au lait" on the table and two slices of bread and butter; he takes the two ten franc coins that I fish out of my pocket and gives me one franc twenty change. Somebody comes in.

The Street

I was walking down this street, straight and sloping away from the sun, between cars moving with a vague slowness. Walking down this street I had a sense of the past, a distant past, a different street. I was unable to retrace my steps back to it. Not in person, not in reflections thrown from windows: in certainty to retrace it, only in certainty. When I'd be in the past of that other street I'd know it. But how?

That street, which was not this street, how could it be here again, how show itself to me while I was walking, pursued by sun, by the flickering of trees, by swirls of dust? There were three yellow dogs, one bicycle, one bakery. Street without street, full of houses without houses, roofs without roofs. The street of the past, if it came near, if I were able to make it move toward me, how would it appear to me, there, now, past? Still, I made an effort to stir up such astonishment in myself.

A street from time past announced its strange future presence. It would come. It would be the past coming toward me. It would carry through this movement. And what it would show me, no matter how close, would declare itself as elsewhere. By what sign? a label? a voice?

The street of the past was at the end of a path punctuated by way stations: at every station on the path of recollection, an image. Ten, twenty, thirty stations on the path. But no certainty of reaching the end. None. Except that it would be the last station. And that it would be so only once I had, by an effort of memory, placed myself all at once before the penultimate image. Then the past would be, immediate.

The penultimate image was also of a street. It was neither of the street I was walking down now, nor of the one I had walked in the

80

past, which resembled the former, or not, but in any case called out to me. I knew it was the one, the one from before. Liquid street, somber; the same trees; others. But the very moment I knew I ceased knowing.

II

Twenty Sonnets
Six Little Logical Pieces
Square des Blancs-Manteaux: Meditation on Death

Twenty Sonnets

SONNET I

A girl in love, excited, at the Main
Post Office (Louvre) thrusts a letter in
Her fingers tremble and her palms are sweaty
She blushes, hurrying, anxious and troubled.
  But now my curiosity is doubled
On seeing a young man with poe-ets* mane
Waiting outside, continuing to crack
And, one by one, eat peanuts from a pack.
  She heaves a sigh into the dusk. Today
Is Sunday, long Sunday in August, when
Heat grips both town and heart in its dead grip.
  Do I read rightly this uncertain sight?
Unlikely my interpretation's right;
On lover's (?) arm, fair redhead walks away.

---

*Plural, since demi-Rimbaud, demi-Baudelaire.

SONNET II
Square de Louvois

Maybe a thousand times these thirty years
   I've sat on a green bench in Louvois Square
   Sun in my eyes, alone, circled by noises
   From drooling fountains, walked over by voices.
Of jetting water wonders, I myself
   Once had in my possession treasured book(s)
   Recallable, in theory, to their place(s)
   On ex-His Majesty's Library shelf.
Saône, the Seine, the Loire, and the Garonne
   I eyed those river-nymphs, their brimming gaze,
   Mused on their allegorical bronze breasts
Then I recrossed the Rue de Richelieu
   Reclaimed my place and then, euphoric reader,
   King-like enjoyed republican milieu.

Sonnet III

"That afternoon I walked Rue de Bretagne
I often bring to mind that afternoon"
My local Prisunic handcart I soon
loaded with cakes and cider from Mortagne
(Just for example). These department stores
Are earthly paradises. You can find
Butter and candies, marshmallows, scant undies
For ladies, gents, eau de cologne or drawers.

A banal day it was, in banal times
Nothing that happened merited a look
No act worth putting in a history book
It was a day in June, uncomplicated
Which I remember only from those lines
Of Aragon that popped into my mind.

SONNET IV
In This City You Didn't Love

Here in this city you don't love
In which you've passed so many days
That counting makes you want to puke
Afraid of things unrecognized!

Afraid of everything you've seen!
Crossing the streets and then recrossing
The muddy ways, the ways of snow
Ways of the tongue-tied, sullen masks

Here in this city you don't love
City you'll never get out of
Because of all you still don't know

Summerfuls of syllabic tasks
Dazed by your dead who died right here
Here in this city you don't love

Sonnet V
Endgame

As summer comes around for one last (?) time
You take its books back to the BIBLIOTHÈQUE
DE LA SORBONNE. For twenty, thirty years
Perhaps a thousand times,* each time more fears
You've climbed the squeaky-sounding wooden stairs
Uncertain until fifth, sixth, seventh floors
Of *Building B.* You've gazed out on a roof
In the medieval light of windows sealed.
Your arms grown heavy with a heavy ration
Of will-to-know, you have, to quench your passion
For the unknown that wells up from such paper
Topped willy-nilly off your towering pile
With one more, chosen not according to
Warburg's "good neighbor" principle, but

By chance.
— And . . . ?
— No luck.

---

*Cf. Sonnet II, line 1.

Sonnet VI

Space statuated in pale marble, park
   Bestrewn with leaves, lovers, and children floating
   What they think are uncapsizable boats:
   "NEC MERGITUR!" O clipper *Cutty Sark.*
The Sun, more evanescent than the snark,
   Disperses dustily—the chestnuts drown—
   Yellow, a color-up, where well-bathed sparrows
   Debauch beneath nude Eros's well-hung bow.
Automobilized Paris rolls its din:
   Fires, flares, and cries burn, claw, and overthrow
   A sky exacerbated, curving west.
Fountains fling up their water far and wide
   Which flies in murmurs, humbled by the heft
   Of gravity: wind, water—misallied.

SONNET VII
To the Eiffel Tower

All right now, Eiffel Tower, stop giving me the eye like that.
If I present you with a sonnet in correct fourteeners
(A meter Jacques Réda has toiled assiduously at)
It doesn't give the right to meter me with your crabbed eye

Meters you have, it's true, and also have the color drab
(I think the French would call it "terne") in common with the crab
In spite of the Mercurochrome (lead oxide, red) with which
The city disinfects your scratches from the wind and sand.

A dense crowd amble in the area your four legs straddle
And gawk up at your nether parts. Should you not hide your ass?
(Ass theoretical, it's true) but children are not banned

And will go back directly to our countryside and dream
Perverted ever after—love, but for a giantess
Like quite unquiet hamlets lying at the mountain's foot.

Sonnet VIII
Gare Saint-Lazare

Long years ago the train to Bois-Colombes
At midnight carried off my then-beloved.
Her lips, her breasts set me on fire, but still
The waiting room preserved a graveyard chill.

Unquiet day of an unquiet time
When the Long March had barely reached its goal
I was eighteen. The shadow of that struggle
Lowered upon the love that fired my brain

Because my love was, more than she was mine,
Chinese (her father's side) and Mister T.
Prepared to break Western connections now

And rally to the side of Chairman Mao.
So that I saw us, both Miss T. and me,
In China, at the Great Wall, laying bricks.

SONNET IX
Rue Rossini

Rossini's street elbows and it's a green
Saucer holds the torn check for my café
Au lait. Reflections, sodden, daub a June
cloudscape upon somebody's open window

The floor above the antique store. Air mild,
The morning quiet, certainly I could
Read, think, or dream—ah, but my cheeky ears
Prefer to eavesdrop on the neighborhood.

Lifting her nude arms, tanned, the brunette beauty
Says (and her armpits, by the way, show promise):
"But I'm a human being, not a dog!"

Her interlocutor seems quite perplexed
(Such conversations have text and subtext):
"You should say 'bitch'." To which comes no reply.

Sonnet X
Canal Saint-Martin

One side of the canal is Quay Valmy
And Quay Jemmapes is on the other. You
decide to take a break, sit on a bench
A while, across from the half-open lock.

Water cascading throws out such a roar
The traffic's roar's diminished to a sigh
Hands on your knees and eyes on the dark water
Unmoving you sit there while time goes by

Then you will go across the footbridge whose
Image completes an oval in the water
Pale out-of-focus plane trees, pale leaves fallen,

Submerged in endless pale colorless sky.
The barge *Robert* comes from the tunnel under
The bridge. Water foams up to the sluice doors.

SONNET XI
Sunday, mein Oberkampf

Bus 20 for Filles-du-Calvaire where CRÊP-
ERIE MORGANE abuts LULU BERLU
(*Open from noon to 9, to 3 on Sundays*)
Rue Oberkampf gives on Boulevard Voltaire.

HOTEL ATLANTIS I allow a glance
While on a bench, Boulevard Richard-Lenoir
LINGERIE FABIOLA, VILLA D'UDINE (*pizza*),
AVIV GIFTS—DISCOUNT (*dishes, toys for kids*)

Rues Jacquard, de Nemours, (new-)Popincourt
LUX PRESSING, PAMELA PERFUMES, then Par-
mentier I cross, where there's a THUNDER BAR.

A few steps farther old CAFÉ CHARBON
Remodeled strictly in nostalgic style
Not nuisancing the neighboring MCDONALD'S

Line 29

To the end of the line for sheer pleasure

On little pebbles the large leaves collapse
Already. Ping-pong[1] tables are set up
(Fake marble tops and all) I'm welcomed by
Roses aglow with early morning dew.

I've come some distance.[2] Reuilly I passed through
And Picpus, with brisk step and wary eye
To annotate the streets cut up by high-
Ways, with potholes, dumpsters, winches and cranes.

Pretty soon I'll know every bench in town
I notice cigarette butts, tickets,[3] ants[4]
A fallen crow—cantankerous, uncivil.

Once my account's[5] complete, I'll follow plans
Buy butter and some pepper (well, *du poivre*)
All to be found[6] at Porte de Montempoivre

---

[1] And two miniature football games. Two *baby-foot!*
[2] From Saint-Lazare.
[3] Bus or Métro, used.
[4] New.
[5] Of details.
[6] In a GAM ("the night owl shops").

Sonnet XIII
Rue Bobillot

The axeman's block
Shiny in satin
The raw blade: that in
Rue Bobillot

Fish eyes blink more
Than the folk who watched
The head detach
From old Adam Billaut.

Onomastics (handmaid)
Unreasonably offers
Me this macabre scene

From one fate never fazed,
Poet of *Vilebrequin**
Which Pierre Corneille praised.

---

*And let us not forget *Les chevilles* [The Pegs], the first work of this carpenter poet from Nevers (1602-62).

SONNET XIV

Suspicion rests on Rue Bezout
   A crisis of identity
   Nobody sells potatoes there
   No seeping fuel-oil (Fr. *mazout*)
Every façade, it seems, is keen
   On sedentary set routine
   No mystery, well yes but comfort
   On this numb dumb August 13.
O Tombe-Issoire, my Tombe-Issoire
   Farewell, you Folie-Méricourt
   You'd just find yourself in the way
Soon there won't be enough sky left
   To take these white lead clouds that fall
   And cover us beyond recall.

Sonnet XV

A little redhead in Park Georges-Brassens
Welcomes the droplets on her red dress, till
Wind shifts the fountain's watery cool veil
To chase after some ducks caught in its spill.

The bar *Dupont Convention* serves white beer
From Bruges and with an added lemon twist
It's through the porte Brancion that we got here
Eyes red from all the dust. It's Sunday now.*

The farthest farness of my walk would be
The last uneven number, 407
Rue Vaugirard which comes to kick the bucket

Shunting its sidewalks underneath some tracks
No longer used. The entrance: wooden door
With plaque: PODIATRY AND PEDICURE.

---

*Again (cf. sonnet I: this Sunday, one suspects, came before the one in the poem that precedes it in this book).

SONNET XVI
Maison de la Radio

Door Ay, Door Bee, Door See, Door Dee, Door Ee
Door Eff, a dreary evening in May
I turn one way and then try retrograde
Door Eff, Ee, Dee, See, Be, Ay (hey hey!) Bee,

See, Dee, et ketera, my firm footsteps
Disturb the pigeons. Not impossible
That after seven times around I'll get
To the appointment I'm supposed to keep.

I wander every radial passageway,
Find studios by doors you don't go in.
I must have got the hour wrong (week wrong?) (day?)

Silence of corridors. Its fractal seconds
Red dots melting away. A minute dies
While I stand here, thinking up vain replies.

Sonnet XVII

That unimportant day, Rue de Saussure
Slowly I walked, lest I forget myself,
Sat on a bench next to a poplar, stared
Downward contemplatively straight at my

Right shoe. Above, bright in a wounded sky,
The August sun threw down its photons on
A million dusty leaves. Without a blink
I met its glare, risking a dizzied head.

Christine de Pisan—well, the city fathers
Have not exactly spoiled her in their planning:
Her street turns out an end more or less dead.

Square Paul-Paray I stumbled onto next.
A cloud passed over. Fast as rules allowed
Rail West trains charged that seaslug-colored cloud.

Sonnet XVIII

In Avenue Junot lived Theodore
    Fraenkel. One visit I remember, from
    A trunk in back he pulled out a Magritte,
    An Ernst, a Miró (star and mandola).
All through our lunch he talked of Isidore
    (Ducasse), of Aragon, Breton et al.,
    Desnos, Crevel, the dead who on recall
    Shine like dark paintings sunlight turns to gold.
In his kitchen one day we glimpsed an old
    Friend of his, Georges Bataille by name, who drank
    Red wine and whose face was sublimely pink.
His hand was shaky, battling with the bottle.
    As we were leaving, Theodore gave Sylvia
    The Blue of Noon, "My dear," he said, "read it.
    It is a novel fresh and exquisite."

SONNET XIX
Buttes-Chaumont

O nature—sentimental! Baby carriages!
cascade! trails with the bushes twisted by
cement! like fading sound from steps of long
ago, trails longer than a black swan's neck,
white under wings, downy like daddy's beard,
just where to poke your little-girl-all-dressed-
up tongue! and pink all over with pink sugar!
cold pushes us to Marigny—the waiter

complains, "some May Day this!" I tell him that
it snowed in forty-five on May Day. "Well,
that's true" (he must admit—he heard it from
his "sainted!" mother); now holds up a check
on Crédit Lyonnais left by some client
and makes a very negative remark

on public services
since I demur, we go our ways agreeing
to disagree. It's raining.

Sonnet XX

We seat ourselves on rough chairs in this fake
Temple, fake church, fake congregation, nose
Cold, feet cold, fingers cold, cold air sans passion,
sans tears, sans kleenex, sans sobs, sans echoes

The last arrivals have to stand. Enclosed
Quasi-silence leaves only the eyes free
To excavate the garish ceiling vault
Bluer than sea-waves, studded with sham stars.

Incessant waves, a sermon now, in music,
A potpourri of poem, jazz, and Schubert,
Assaults unendingly the public's audi-

Tory canals. We wait to hear the body
Burn in hell's central fires below us, then
We'll realize our friend is truly dead.

It stops now and
Gray gentlemen advance, a box in hand
Much like a box of Bertillon's ice cream.

Six Little Logical Pieces

I

It's Raining

to Charlotte Borel
on the occasion of a certain lack
of hydraulic pressure

— I believe it's raining, but it isn't.
— You believe it's raining and you assert that it is not?
— That's right.
I believe it's raining, but I know I'm wrong.
— How do you know?
— That's not the problem. The problem is: I believe it's raining,
But I'm wrong.
— Who says you are wrong?
— I do.
— But if you are wrong to believe it's raining,
If you know you are wrong to believe it's raining,
How can you believe it's raining?
Give me a straight answer.
— Is it raining?
— No.
— There you are!
— I see that it's not raining. But I don't see how you can
Say you believe it's raining
And how you can
At the same time say this belief is wrong. I can't
Believe it.

— I believe that I believe it's raining and that I know it is not.
— OK.
— If I believe I believe what I believe, then I believe it.

— OK.

— Nobody believes that and at the same time not that.

— That what? not what that?

— Anything: that it's raining, for example.

— Alright.

— If I believe that I'm wrong to believe it's raining,

In other words, if I believe it's raining even though its not the case that it's raining,

It follows that I believe that I believe it's raining

And at the same time that it's not the case that it's raining

And it follows that I believe simultaneously that it's raining

And that it's

Not. But since nobody has ever believed at the same time that it's raining and that it isn't, it's impossible that I should believe that I believe it's raining

While knowing that it is not.

— Indeed.

— And yet I believe it.

— You believe what?

Anyway, it's raining.

Raining!

Raining!

Raining!
Rue des Acacias
des Rasselins
des Lilas

Raining!
Rue Malassis
Saint-Amand

Raining!
Rue Bichat
Brillat-Savarin
de Taïti

Raining!

Raining!
Rue Radziwill
Vic-d'Azir
de la Paix
Jasmin

Raining!

Raining!
Rue Chabanais
Gavarni
Francis-Picabia

Raining!
Rue de Madrid
de Siam
Martignac
Saillard

Raining!
Rue des Anglais
Tristan-Tzara

Raining!
Rue Vavin
Vital
Papin
Paganini

Raining!
Bd. Raspail
Saint-Martin
Raining!

Raining!
Rue Alain
Cabanis
de Navarin

Raining!
Rue de Capri
des Cinq-Diamants

Raining!
Rue Darwin
Jadin

Mignard
de Chablis
du Liban
du Dr.-Babinski

Raining!
Rue Piat
St.-Sabin
de Villafranca

Raining!
Rue de Cambrai
Raining!
Rue Friant
Martin-Garat
de Dantzig
de Milan

Raining!
Rue Chardin
Maillard
des Irlandais
Vivaldi
Ravignan

Raining!
Rue Cail
d'Aix
de Paradis

Raining?
Raining!

II

The Past

She says to him: "Very nice out."
So
it was nice out.
If it's nice out it isn't necessarily very nice out.
If she had said "nice out"
could he have understood her, potentially
in some way
to say
"nice out, *but* not very nice out"?
No.
"Nice out" would not have indicated any reservation on her part.
But neither would he have understood in
"nice out"
(if she had said "nice out")
"nice out, even very nice out."
"Nice out"
would not have indicated
on her part
any insistance.
However if, having said "nice out"
(which had not been the case)
she had added "even very nice"
would this have meant that she thought
that in simply saying
"nice out" she had not been sufficiently precise
had not sufficiently affirmed
how nice it was out?
No doubt.

But could she have said
"nice out, even very nice out"?
No.
Why not?
We don't say that. If she had said
"even very nice out" after having said"very nice out"
she would have applied the operative "even" to the statement
"very nice out." But when you say
"very nice out" you by no means say
nice out, but not very nice,
which you might want to add to the statement "nice out" with as
much likelihood as "even very nice" and it follows that this "even"
is inapplicable
to the statement
"very nice out."

— Really?

And was it nice out?

— It was.

(translated with Norma Cole and Michael Palmer)

A Street

Day breaks

here

light comes

comes again

goes away

where day broke

here

III

The Time of Lightning

To say that it's false to say that lightning is pink
says nothing other than that it's not the case that
lightning is pink
that is to say to say
that lightning is not pink
and this is not
something one would say
of the proposition "lightning is pink" but
a sentence a bit more complicated
about lightning.

In the same way, to say
that X believes lightning is pink
does not mean anything other than
"X believes that
lightning is pink"
or that
"lightning is pink
thinks X,"
which is likewise not
and doesn't even resemble
the proposition "lightning is pink"
but is and resembles a sentence
a bit more complicated
about lightning
and about X.

And yet, summer it was, and evening
and the lightning was blue.

The Time

to On Kawara

It was the time, it was the time, it was the time,
  it was the time, was the time, the time,

and it was the time, and it was the time, and it was the time,
  and it was the time, was the time, the time,

because it's been the time, it's been the time, it's been the time,
  it's been the time, been the time, the time,

that's been the time, that's been the time, that's been the time,
  that's been the time, been the time, the time,

that will have been the time, that will have been the time,
      that will have been the time,
  that will have been the time, been the time, the time,

and stopped being the time, and stopped being the time, and
      stopped being the time,
  and stopped being the time, being the time, the time

of his life,
        his life,
            life.

(translated with Norma Cole and Michael Palmer)

118

IV

The Book

— Hey, here's the book.
Done.
Open it, read.
There.

— "Dear, dearest X,
All that is true in this book I owe to you
All the errors, and there surely are some, are due to my negligence."

You really think so, my dear Y? you sincerely believe there is at least one error in your book?
And that you owe to me all the truth in it?
— Without any doubt, dear, dear X
Are you not my inspi, inspiration, inspirer, the dispen, dispenser of truth?

— You are right, there is at least one.
— One what?
— One error. There is at least one error in your book.
— Where?
— Either what you just made me read is false, is an error, and there is at least that error in your book.
Or what I just read is true, and there is at least one error,
Elsewhere,
In your book.

Let us assume for the moment that this error is elsewhere in the book.

119

If you say in the book this
If you say in the book that,
If you say in the book some other this
If you say in the book some other that,
Et cetera,
Given there is at least one error in the book
It follows that this or that or this other this or this other that or
et cetera
Is false
And consequently since you say in your book
This, that, this other this, this other that and et cetera
Your book, considered as a whole,
Is a tissue of contradictory affirmations, and is
logically impossible.
— But . . .
— And if all you say in the book
Including what you say to me at the beginning of the book
You say because you sincerely believe it
Not only is what you say inconsistent
But what you believe is also.
Under these conditions I prefer
Not to be part of your book.

— Nevertheless I've said at least something true in my book.
Because I can prove rigorously
Using only propositional calculus and
(Classical)
Quantification theory
That if I, Y, have said in my book
That something I have said in my book
Is false
Then something I have said in my book
Is false

And the assertion that there is falsity in my book
Is true.
Let us, dear X, informally assume
That this assertion
I.e. that there is at least one error in my book
Is false
Then *this* will be false
There will be, falsely, *that*
In the book
The attempt to falsify the assertion
That there is something false in my book
Is self-destructive
The only thing it can be
Is true
And this unsuspected
Unanswerable, inextinguishable truth
Is the very truth that I owe you and I offer you,
Dear X.

— Perhaps. But let's assume
That you've been too modest.
Let's assume
(After all this book is your life's work
You have spent much time on it
You've started from first principles
You've deduced the being and nonbeing of the world,
And love that moves heaven and the stars
And time and memory and number and thought,
And many more things)
Let us assume, I say,
That *all* you have said in the book
Up to those words addressed to me
Is true,

Then, since you tell me there is something false in what you say
in the book
And since this assertion
Which can be rigorously proved by logical calculus
Can only be true,
It is false.

I will tell you this, my dear Y,
In yet another way.
It is not possible to say
In a book
That something said in this book
Is false
Unless something other than this assertion is asserted in the
book
And is false.
Certainly in a book
Where only true things are asserted
Or in a book where nothing at all is asserted
Anybody can inscribe or have inscribed
The sentence
"Something is said in this book
that is false"
But one cannot without contradiction assert in the book
That something asserted *in the book*
Is false.
I, you, he, anyone can say this elsewhere
In an interview,
On TV,
And it will be false
But one *cannot* say it
In the book.

— And what if I put
All this
All we've just said
In the book?

A Street

To suffer
really suffer
suffer this end of the street
and those liquids
windows
pulled down
along the street
to suffer
with the eyes
hand
against the stone

the light

        there

the light

        there

and the street

between

V

The Occasion

I hadn't been able to think
on this particular occasion
either erroneously
or correctly

on this particular occasion
I couldn't think
that I was in error
that something I'd thought
on this occasion
was false
without also thinking
that on this particular occasion
I'd also thought something else
that was false

and I couldn't have been afraid
on this particular occasion
with reason or without
when this something of which I had been afraid
on this particular occasion
was not something I could be afraid of
reasonably

I couldn't have been afraid of what had frightened me
if I hadn't
on this particular occasion
been afraid

of something completely different, some other un-
reasonable fear.

I would so have wanted
to have only one thought and one fear only
and for no particular occasion, no hazardous privation
    of these possibilities, to shield me from
what would come, depriving me of them forever

fear
fear
fear

A Street

from the bed of the street
come
came
plumb
these clouds
so plumb
it was impossible
not possible the street
had not steered them
impossible

that even at night
come
came
these clouds
on a course
so exactly like that of the street
all by themselves
(so plumb
a course
it was

scary)

VI

The Truth

— Nothing holds me back
from thinking one single
thing namely that I think
something.

— Nothing indeed
not
if you think you
think nothing but
that, then
truly
you think true.

— But I'd like
to think truth
here and now
not think of anything
in this floating world
this fallible world
this rotten plank of a world
to think
truth truly
pure truth
I want
to think nothing other
than this:
what I think
is true.

— And you'd be thinking what?

— Well, nothing but:
"What I think
is true."

— You can't

you can't think
that what you think there
if that's what you're thinking
is true
the truth of what you think
presupposes that what you think true
is true
but since you are only thinking one thing
which is that you think something
true
the truth of what you think
depends on the truth
of what you're thinking
and you'll never be able
to decide.

— What can I do?

— Think
that *something else*
is true
something in the world
that is not
this thought.

— What are you thinking?

— I'd like to think
there's someone
in this room
but I don't know
that it's true.

A Street

I'm still alive

I walk
as if every house either
side of the street lit up by the
temporal policeman's flashlight
were a point
in the eternal sequence
of before and after
while I walk
the moving street
but when the light
rounds the corner at the drugstore where a
tree once listed, and a bicycle, and a dog

I'm still alive

Square des Blancs-Manteaux, 1983
Meditation on Death, in Sonnets
According to the Protocol of Joseph Hall

I The Entrance — II The Description — III The Division — IV The Causes — V The Effects — VI The Subject —

VII The Adjuvant — VIII The Contrary — VIIII The Comparisons — X The Names — XI The Testimonies — XII The Taste of our Meditation —

XIII The Complaint — XIIII The Wish — XV The Confession — XVI The Petition and Enforcement — XVII The Assurance or Confidence — XVIII The Thanksgiving —

I

The Entrance

Death's entrance, as you enter in, dissent,
  Decenter Death's dementia and her sense,
  From Death's Senses, absent thee and resent
Consenting to Death's constant Constancy.
By Death passed by, repent and be content
  When Death is pending, her Lamp and her stamp,
  Clamber toward Death, approach and accent her,
Think yourself Death's indecency and temple.
Death readying to carry you away
  Transport Death in amphorae, deport Death
Aggress your Death, baseless and faceless Death
And when in dread of Death, make haste: unlace,
  But bow down when Death is discredited
Think how All-wearied Death gives touch, gives bed.

II

The Description

Black sheet, dead woman white, reversing light
   Since Death comes changing day's black and day's white
   The bird lamp turns to cinders with a hiss
   I see fingers, some blood the Sun pours down
By this reversal Death has promised never
   To leave me anything that's calm or sure
   The mirror's surface sets the wall afire
   But no breath's clouding it because she ceases
She ceases while asleep; the past, departing,
   Empties the ashtray, for this instant cancels
   Entitlement to color and to silence
And then I see her eyes move that will close
   That, closing, have closed more than time, a room
   More than a bed, more than a tree, a tomb.

III

The Division

Sad sod and mud, brutal and brusque rebuff
Humid, humble, fixed in deaf heavy turf
The ground ground down to crumb in curves and crust
Mixed muted matte all flustered in its falling

Acrid wrack sunk in vile miserly mooring
Cave tainted, entangled, quite done for, strangled
Body still proper washed of bile and slaver
Grave body made more grave in Earth, Cadaver.

Then Death divides the Bodies she ingests
Making their eyes into holes, their legs halt
Grinds hollow their bones, their tongues, their gestalt

Death non-divides only skull, only dust
Death stows away in gunnies, in her fist
A manifold of instants clipped from Earth.

IV

The Causes

The coming second is the Cause of Death
Death will have come and Death would have already
Tarnished the retina, hardened the hand.
The coming second will collapse your Body.
   The second to come, "Death!" will have changed "Sleep!"
From a familiar word to far off, mute.
In Cause of Death, the coming second will
Against the sheets arrest your leaden Body,
   The Death-snatched Body, the same moment share
With your tanned belly, naked, live with life,
That breathed in dawn's red world of air,
   The throb of time, echo before the sound,
Resin from no tree, night night overtaking,
Sole Cause of Death the next second succeeding.

V

The Effects

The second that was was the Effect of Death:
  Death was to come and Death would take good care
  To drain your eyes, asphyxiate your hands.
  The second that was was to crush your Body
By Death's Efforts effected; and then Death,
  Squashing your eyeballs in her fist-tight clench,
  Second that was, the next second Death's wrench-
  Ing change, marking the Body's quick disaster:
That Body Death desired to leave unborn
  Having been never, wedged in ever faster
  Flickers of time, blips between sap and rind,
Day-night, past-future, World and World-no-more,
  As if Nothing that was were your World ever.
  The second that was was her Strength's Effect.

VI

The Subject

Subject to Death you are
Spread on the ground your goods
Cards, letters, snapshots, words
Of your own Death you're Subject
Body bodiless you
Losing your lips, your words
Earth's black hair at the edge
Of an unbordered Death
Here a present is held
That you'll not hold, that you
Give leave to ply its target.
There no minding imposs-
Ibles or possibles
Your Death the other Subject.

VII

The Adjuvant

Why do you shift, light, on this wall
In silences, on screens, confusions
Emblems and hieroglyphs, in fissions,
Volume and character, in sheer
   Calamity? Why, light, these visions,
Perfect companions to all bright
Sky in or outside me, my future's
Loop, thanks to your slow profusion?
   Why, light, throw me, so worn, the shadow
Under her lids, rife with the sure
concussion of refracted night—
   So I will see but vitreous humor
Of eyes turned sightless to the wall?
That and the present light—no, rather plural: *lights*?

VIII

The Contrary

In victory, death forces Death to spurn
  All fire, all water, all earth, and all air.
  In Death's despite your death is ordinary,
  Death's tryout death, a Death-exempted death,
An allegory Death speaks in your death
  Rejecting any voluntary frill:
  No consolation, no thought, and no prayer
  In other words, not Death, but just your death.
It's not denying it to repeat, "life,
  Your shifting shape surviving among trees,
  Always again these shutters shut you out"
And maybe in the dregs of calm we'd seize
  Day at the height of day, its true routines,
  How confines fall, and vestiges, and cards.

VIIII

The Comparisons

Like hair : dark like forehead : black like
Eye : black and eye : black like lash : black
And neck : dark like mouth : shadowed like
Tooth : whence double : lip : black like cheek :
Black like back : dark like armpits : dark :
Black like breasts : dark breast-hers : dark-dark :
Sweet like skin : dark like rump : dark under
Black cloth like fur : black around black

Like dark or down dark belly : dark
Thighs of shadow : knee black like shadow
Hands : shadows of hands : black of hands :
Dark black like black of bones : dark shadow
Like lying down : dark at night : dark
Like your death : dark like dark like : nothing.

X

The Names

Death's Names we say without an echo:
Isle! Elm! Alarm! Oar! Rhyme! End! Weft!
Lex! King! Retreat! Tea! and still others,
Words to belabor till what's left

Is Nothing, indivisible,
Material, proper, Death's Names Super-
Proper, all, without fine or chime,
Fixed sempiternel by the moment.

The Names for Death: bereft, things, knot
Ubiquitous, dropped swap, solo,
Tough; solipsistic Death's sons, daughters.

Memory speaks them, night distracted,
Nature so fitting, so distracted,
Distracted you, among Death's Names.

XI

The Testimonies

The stars have as their Judge the God of Lights
    Who in hard purity outdoes the Sun,
    Such *cruel* Principle, clear cruelty,
    Immobile Witness in its red ellipses.
High hand of lightning, where the luminaries
    Dash the impurities of their cold load.
    What silly furor out of endless Blindness
    Can make you treasure Death in your own void?
My heart has place for no shred of belief
    In all your demonstrations! Ah, if lent
    From you some residue of old time faith,
Would I be soothed, Fictional Firmament?
    Or left to undergo Sisyphus's grief,
    Caught in your furrow ploughed by witches' breath?

XII

The Taste of our Meditation

Nothing's Seen here but Earth in Earth
  Scattered squadron of many dead
  Blood-sangria has dyed the Earth
  Death makes the end too deep to sound
Nothing is Heard here, Earth on Earth
  But wind, its tongue rustling around
  Gravestones; Smell, there's the Smell of Earth
  Stale smoke from rubble and old leaves
Add to Sight Hearing, and to Hearing
  Smell—prize these senses in descending
  Order and know: from sky to earth
That your task or your mission's Death
  Down there, your mouth choked up with ash,
  To Touch Hell in your Meditation.

XIII

The Complaint

No complaint, walking, no more crying,
No thinking, never talking any more,
No more, but walk no longer sighing
The spiral letdown of the hours, these hours.
Not fearful any longer, walking,
Asleep upright, of nothing, nothing, steps,
Some other; opening your eyes
There's nothing, nothing there, a dog, a flower.
You don't think to complain, to yell
You let yourself sink in the sea of
Your moments, all blank, in between clear bounds
One by one worn away. Your hand
Traces no name now on each frosted
Pane. You complain no more. Thus you complain.

XIIII

The Wish

At last, at last away from so much Death
  So much invariance of grass and tears
  Such overflow of horror, such alarm,
  Determined to keep nothing, nothing stirring,
So many days and nights engaged in chasing
  After a thread misplaced among the wefts
  Of body and of soul not yet unsnarled,
  At last, at last quitting so much of Death
To reach, at last, within some solitude
  Nearby,   at last, at last, sinking
  In blessed dullness down to mute unthinking
At last

XV

The Confession

This. this. branches moved. steps. lost steps.
two. this. words. wordless. the words gone
numb. white noise. mouth sealed. this. forsaken
false peace. this. this. refused. withdrawn.
To fall. this. fall. fall say. illsaid.
points. drop. break the true. contradict.
a ruse. this. move. elude. strict law of
finger on mouth. scared days. nights. nights.
So this. return. recall. invisible.
deaf. without smell. taste. touch. abstract.
flat. nude. not done. doubtful. intact.
So. there. called to say. hurried. answer
your question: nothing can be done?
Answer. this: nothing can be done.

XVI

The Petition and Enforcement

Erase this night invested with her Death
Erase this dawn accomplice to her Death
Erase this tightly locked door of her Death
Erase this room disheveled by her Death

Erase these curtains pulled across her Death
Erase this waking lived in by her Death
Erase this mirror clouded with her Death
Erase this sun on the floor of her Death

Erase this hand still barely warm in Death
Erase this mouth that was poisoned by Death
Erase this eye that turned to wood in Death

Break in upon this Death, bury this Death
Intimidate this Death, knock down this Death
Take this Dead Woman to her lasting Death.

XVII

The Assurance or Confidence
Silence : Rue : Silence

Conceivable the silence that in silence
   Is, and if filled with no noise, even white,
   Empty (same thing?) from the same empty place,
   That the point of an echo bound or balance.
Silence, therefore, a bastion of untravel,
   Of uncolor as well, the tacit end
   Of music waiting for a subtle heart
   Where pain and the immense could reconcile.
Silence around the silence of a trace
   To see as far as your mind's night, which is
   The wave exonerated from its spume:
Parenthesis opened against a time
   When, at the same time, same and other open
   Left for silence to close and to exhume.

XVIII

The Thanksgiving

Give thanks: to Someone, whoever. Give thanks
    Also to That which is No-one. Whether
    For Nothing, for a Thing, or for Another.
    We owe thanks to: the nail, the cat, vanilla.
For moments of discernment, thanks. A thousand
    Telling details: thank you. There is no why,
    Neither from need, nor by some moral law's
    Effect within a heart. Just render thanks.
From your Thanksgiving by no means exclude
    The day of wrath. Say: "I give thanks to Death.
    I give Death thanks and at her fountain die
Of joy in enjoying her stranglehold,
    to spew out her thought, make her magnet turn,
I give my thanks to Death, great peneplain,

And have done with thoughts thinking of her Death."

III

Reading the Streets
Hommage to Sébastien Bottin's Telephone Directory
Songs of Streets and Streets
Quiet Days at the Porte d'Orléans
Undated Night, Rue Saint-Jacques

Reading the Streets

The Streets in Paris

The streets in Paris have two sides
that's a general rule

There is no street in Paris that has no sides
(besides I don't see how there could be a street in Paris (or else-
where) that has no sides)
There's not one street in Paris with only one side
(besides I don't see how there could be a street in Paris (or else-
where) with only one side)
it would be difficult for a street in Paris to have three sides
a street in Paris could very well have four sides
You'd only have to build houses in the middle of an ordinary street
with two sides
however this is not done
in short
the streets in Paris have two sides

The streets in Paris have houses on each side
that's a general rule
if a street in Paris doesn't have houses on one side
and if on the other side is the Seine
then it's not a street but a quay
Rue de Médicis has no houses on the side of the Luxembourg
Gardens
Rue de Lutèce not either (on the side of the Arènes de Lutèce)
nor Rue Cuvier along the Botanical Garden
in this case
we shall say with Gawanna in the Nyâya-sûtra, that a street has

157

non-houses on the side where it doesn't have houses and that these
non-houses are characterized by the non-presence of houses
on that side of the street
which is by no means a negative observation
just as an absence of noise is nothing other
than a positive observation of silence

and if a street in Paris has no houses on either side
then there are non-houses on either side of the street

The streets in Paris have a left side and a right side
like us
the left side of a street in Paris is the one where the uneven house
numbers go up on your left as you walk
the right side of a street in Paris is the one where the even house
numbers go up on your right as you walk
that's a general rule
(when I walk in a street in Paris I make sure to check if this
condition is satisfied
(a condition that would not hold for the houses of the town of
Reus in Catalonia
where the arrangement is the opposite
as good a way as any for this town to affirm its singularity
(in Caunes-Minervois all the houses of the town are numbered in
one single sequence
so that there is no left or right side in any street
(if you transport all the houses of Caunes-Minervois to Califor-
nia and line them up in ascending order of numbers you get a new
town you can call Caunes-Minervois (Cal.) which will have only one
street, a street with only one side—and without need to suppose some
bizarre topology like a Moebius strip
(if transport seems too costly you could simply construct facsimiles,
as has been done for the Parthenon in Nashville. And, as in Nash-

ville, where the statues missing from the frieze of the Parthenon have been replaced so that the replica should be more authentic than what is left of the original, nothing would keep you from replacing missing tiles on the roofs of the models of houses of Caunes-Minervois (Cal.)

(or even from adding, if desired, a patio in front and a swimming pool in back

(since it's definitely only the house number that counts

(but it will unfortunately not be possible to roll out a strip of asphalt before the houses because then the street would have a second side)))))))

and if it happens that a street in Paris has numbers on only one side

depending on the evenness of numbers this side will be the left (or the right)

and the non-houses on the other side will all bear an absence of number which will be odd if their side is the left and even if it is not

I must admit that streets without houses
and streets that have only houses without numbers
make me wonder

but I'll stop this poem here because of its length
even though there is still much to say about the streets in Paris

Invitation to the Voyage

To m. b.

—Think how nice it would be
to go down there, to go

to Abbeville

to Aboukir, to Ajaccio,

to Alençon, to Alésia, to Alexandria,

to Algiers, the Alps, Alsace-Lorraine, Latin-America, Amsterdam,
Angoulême, Anjou, Anvers, the Apennines, Aquitaine, Arcole,
Arcueil, the Ardennes, to Argenteuil,
to visit
Argentina, Artois, Athens, the Atlas, Aubervilliers, the Aude, the
Aurès, Austerlitz, Auteuil, the Auvergne, the Aveyron,
Babylon, Barcelona, the Béarn, the Beaujolais and Beaune regions,
Belfort, Belzunce,
—Belzunce?
—Yes, Belzunce
Bergamo, Bern, Béthune, the Bidassoa,

There, all is order and beauty
Luxurious calm and delight

Ah how nice to go
to go there, to go
to Bigorre, Blaye, Briare, to Brazil, Bresse, Brittany, Brussels, Bu-
carest, Budapest, Buenos Aires, Cadix, Cahors, Cairo, Cambodia,

to Cambrai, Canada, the Cannebière, to Capri, Casablanca, Castellane, the Cévennes, to Chablis, Chambéry, Chantilly, Charente, Chartres, Châtillon, Cherbourg, Cherche-Midi, Chevreuse, Clairvaux, Clichy,

Clisson, Coëtlogon, Colmar

on the canals afloat
to see the sleeping boats
whose mood is vagabond

& Compiègne, Copenhagen, Corrèze, Corsica/Corse, Cotentin, Costa Rica, Crédit lyonnais, Crimea/Crimée, Croisic, Cronstadt, to Dahomey, Dantzig, the Dardanelles, the Delta
—What delta?

—Dijon, the Dordogne, Douai, Dunkerque,
—Dunkerque!
—Europe, Falaise
& Fécamp, & to Finland, Florence, Franche-Comté, to Gabon, Gascony, & Gâtines, Genoa/Gênes, Gergovie, Guadeloupe, Guatemala, Guyana, Guyenne, Le Havre, Jena/Iéna, Ile-de-France, Indochina, Italy, Japan,   and the Jardin des poètes

where
the setting suns
clothe fields and canals
and the whole city
in hyacinth and gold
—As you say
—Kabylia, Labrador, Laos, Lebanon, Liège, London, Lorraine, Lübeck,
Lutèce, Lyon, Mâcon, Madagascar, Marocco, Martinique, Médoc,

Meaux, Metz, Milano, Minervois, Montauban, Montevideo, Nantes, Narbonne, Nemours, New York, Nevers, Nicaragua, the Niger, Normandie, Odessa, Oran, Oslo, Padirac, Palestine, Parma, Peking, Peru,

Pondichéry, Port-au-Prince, Prague, Presbourg, Provence, the Pyrenees, Rambouillet, Reims, Rennes, the Dominican Republic, the Equatorial Republic, Réunion, Rivoli, Romainville, Rome, Roubaix, Rouen, Roussillon, Sahel, Saint-Gervais, Saint-Mandé, Saint-Maur, Saint-Quentin, Saintonge, Savoy, Salonika, Sebastopol, Senegal, Sfax, Siam,

Solferino, Sudan, Stockholm; Strasbourg, Tangiers, Teheran, Thionville, Timbuktu, Transvaal, Turino, Ulm, Uruguay, Uzès, Valenciennes, Valmy, Valois, Vaucluse, Vauvenargues, the Vendée, Vendôme, Venice, Venezuela, Versailles, Vézelay, Vienna, Vincennes, Ventimiglia, Virginia, Vivarais, Wagram, Washington,

And all that,
— By Orient-Express?
—No,
by Métro, with a simple Orange Card 2 zones

A Bit of Sociology

158 saints, 33 female saints,
popes, 8 cardinals, 11 abbots, 3 abbesses, 1 canoness, 1 rector,
priests, preachers,
Capuchins & Carmelites, Celestines, Recollects
Ursulines, Franciscans,
1 commander-in-chief,

princes, 3 dauphins, 1 princess, 6 counts, 1 countess, knights,
squires,
1 Lord,

4 presidents,

8 marshals, 64 generals, at least 14 colonels, 2 lieutenant-colonels,
    3 commandants, 8 captains, 4 lieutenants, 4 sergeant-majors, 1
    corporal,
crossbowmen,
admirals,

1 agent,

plus 3 judges,

1 banker, entrepreneurs, goldsmiths,
1 single slave trader,

at least 41 doctors,

shepherds—& two shepherdesses,
bons vivants, 2 butchers, bakers,
coal merchants, hunters, lime-burners, vinegar-makers, 1 crêpe-
    maker, 1 cooper, dockers,
1 mailman, 2 mowers, 1 falconer, farmers, landscapers, 1 glazier,
gardeners, sailors, fiddlers, millers,
fish-dealers, 1 haymaker, 1 potter,

4 professors,

painters, poets,

curious, very curious, this distribution
of the population
in the streets
of Paris

Montmartre Cemetery

On the abandoned vault as if a squat for the vagabond dead
nothing left to read but: *Perpetual Care*
(time has peeled off all the names)
among the graves the snails prefer
a novelist could harvest names:

Brunca da Costalorg
Heuzé Miaude
Bouge & Fauvel
Brassac-De Lalaix-Chomeil
Orty de la Roche & Demeuse
Paul Corrude
De Nugent de Dysart & Lemort de la Roche
Chaumereuil
Trimaille
Letteron Rougeron
De Canelaux
Julie Gabrielle Marie Jacqueline des Echards de Sainte Comobe,
    marquise de Fortia
Hocmelle
Alici Lixi
Joachim Lelewel
Barbat de Closel & Petit d'Avril
de Peindrey d'Hurbelle

not to forget Kerudat de Belzim

Doggies and Beauty

Rue Championnet: *History of Bones*
Bow-wow Shop, Rue du Ruisseau
Tick & Flea, Avenue de Saint-Mandé

House of Flasks
Brunny-Facial, at Porte de Montmartre
Cybèle, Rue du Roule, Rue Galande
                    Avenue de Saint-Mandé

"voluminous glamour, the mascara that makes your lashes twice as
    voluminous"

"mirror, hast ever known volume this glamorous"
                    (could be fragment of *Le roman d'Alexandre:*
                    21 August 1997 —Saint-Lazare Station —
                    on the back of bus 24)

Wooden Paris

escalators (Place d'Italie station, and?)
paving (?)

foot bridges (Buttes-Chaumont, and?)
balconies (10 Rue Fessart, and?)
"Wood and Coal Shops" (getting very rare)

benches, gates (passim)
trees
(in Paris the trees are generally of wood)

The Trade in Classics

Cars enter Rue Corneille
Coming from Rue de Vaugirard or Rue Médicis
Cars leave Rue Corneille by the Place de l'Odéon

Cars enter Rue Racine
Coming from Boulevard Saint-Michel or Rue des Écoles
Some turn left onto Rue Monsieur-le-Prince
Cars leave Rue Racine by the Place de l'Odéon

Cars enter Rue La Bruyère
Coming from Rue Moncey
Or down Rue Blanche
Some leave by Rue Henner (to the left)
Others drive up Rue Pigalle
Others take Rue La Rochefoucauld
Cars get to the end of Rue La Bruyère
Some go up Rue Notre-Dame-de-Lorette
Others go down it
Still others drive into Rue Henri-Monnier

Cars enter the first block of Rue Boileau
Coming from Boulevard Exelmans
They go up the street and down the house numbers
Some turn into Rue Molitor (left or right)
Cars leave Rue Boileau by Rue d'Auteuil

Cars enter Rue La Fontaine
Coming from Rue de l'Assomption

Or from Rue de Boulainvilliers
Or from Rue Raynouard
Some turn right onto Avenue du Recteur-Poincaré
Some turn left onto Rue Agar
Others are swallowed by Villa Patrice-Boudarel (a dead end)
Some cars turn left onto Rue François-Millet
Others, left too, onto Avenue de l'Abbé-Roussel
Or onto Rue du Père-Brottier, Rue des Perchamps or Rue Georges-
    Sand (on the right, like Rue du Général-Largeau)
Cars leave Rue La Fontaine. They drive off by Rue Poussin or
    Avenue Mozart
Cars enter Rue Molière
Coming from Rue Richelieu
Or Rue Thérèse
Cars quit Rue Molière by the Avenue de l'Opéra
It's the only way.

aide social	*boule blanche* *boule rouge*	*boule rouge*
campagne première	*chêne vert* *chemin vert*	*chemin vert*
cheval blanc	*cité universitaire* *fonds verts*	*croix rouge*
	grosse bouteille *haut pavé* *haut fonds*, high bottoms is for obvious reasons inappropriate even more so *jardin des poètes*	
forge royale	*immeubles* *industriels* *légion étrangère*	*maison* *blanche*

maison blanche	*maison brûlée*	*missions étrangères*
	moulin vert	
nations unies	*palais royal*	*panier fleuri*
	parc royal	
port royal	*port royal*	*port royal*
	portes blanches	

I'm leaving the XVIIIth
and the letter p
no r, no s
I am afraid
I'm soon
running out
of streets

terre neuve	*ville neuve*	xxxxxxxxxxx
	xxxxxxxxxxxxxxx	

ah! treacherous city!
to leave me in the
lurch a few steps
from the end
of this "elementary
morality"

	saint pères	
sacré coeur	*petits pères*	*petits hôtels*
	petits champs	
petits carreaux	*petites écuries*	*petit truand*
	petite boucherie	
petite arche	*petit pont*	*petit musc*

I hope there'll
   soon be enough
   petite streets
   in *petite*
   corners to finish
   this "elementary
   immorality"

	petit moine	
petit modèle	*petit château*	*petit cerf*
	ouf!	

Counting Out Rhyme for the Year (Two) Thousand

Impasse of the TWO angels
Street of the THREE sisters
Street of the FOUR sons
Street of the FIVE diamond cutters

Street of the SEVEN acres
Street of May EIGHT 1945

Square of June EIGHTEEN 1940

Square of August TWENTY-FIVE 1944

Street of July TWENTY-NINE

Square of June Eighteen 1940

Square of August Twenty-Five 1944

Street of May Eight 1945

Paris, Paris, your city fathers
can't count to 2000

Rainbow

it's raining

it stops raining

it's nice

the sun's shining
you can see

on Rue VIOLET

on Rue BLEUE
on Rue du Chemin-VERT

on Place du Château-ROUGE

a rainbow full of holes

Calculation

The Impasse du BŒUF is in the IVth
in the Vth the Impasse des BŒUFS
goes from the singular ox to the plural
as we jump up one arrondissement

but

Avenue du BOIS is in the XVIth
and it's in the XIXth we find Rue des BOIS
with wood we jump three arrondissments

why?

Rue d'	A i x
Rue	A b e l
Rue	V i è t e
Rue	C o u c h e
Rue	A c h i l l e
Rue	C o r i o l i s
Rue	C o n d o r c e t
Rue d'	A l e x a n d r i e
Rue des	H a u d r i e t t e s
Rue	B a s s o m p i e r r e
Rue	C h a t e a u b r i a n d
Rue de	C o n s t a n t i n o p l e
Rue de	B o u l a i n v i l l i e r s

The Snow is Melting!

Rue de	Boulainvilliers
Rue de	Bretonvilliers
Rue de la	Parcheminerie
Rue	Vauvenargues
Rue de	Steinkerque
Rue	Garancière
Rue des	Alouettes
Rue d'	Alembert
Rue	Laplace
Rue	Albert
Rue	Vilin
Rue	Rude
Cour du	Coq

Plesent Streets

berber berets in *berger street!*
bergs & berms in *bergère street!*
beer in *des bergers street!*

Celts & cells in *cels street!*
cement cepes in *cépré street!*
checkered cheeks in *chevert street!*
clement in *clément street!*
clerks in *cler street!*
credes & credence in *crèche street!*
crests in *cretet street!*

delete *delbet street!*
descend *desgenettes street!*
desert *desprez street!*
drench dresses in *drevet street!*

ebony in *ebelmen street!*
& *eblé street!*
elder eels in *de l'échelle street!*
ere ergs err in *ernest-lefèvre street!*
esteemed in *de l'est street!*
Esther's in *d'estrées street!*
ether ettle in *etex street!*
events ever even in *des évettes street!*

fennel ferments *des fêtes street!*
freckles frequent *fresnel street!*

germs in *gerbert street!*
jests in *gervex street!*
green grebe greed in *de grenelle street!*
greek greegrees in *grenet street!*

Hellenes hellbent in *hélène street!*
then henpecked in *henner street!*
Hermes in *hermel street!*
hertz in *herschel street!*
& *de hesse street!*

jennets jet in *jenner street!*

kelp keeps well *keller street!*
kestrels in *kepler street!*

these lecterns in *leclerc street!*
get left in *lefebre street!*

these legends in *legendre street!*
the length of *leneveux street!*
these lepers in *leredde street!*
these lesser letters of *de lesseps street!*
these level leverets of *levert street!*

the messes of *de metz street!*
the meter of *meyerbeer street!*

the nerve! *de nesle street!*
nevertheless, *de nevers street!*

pecked *peclet street!*
peeled pêle-mêle *pelée street!*

perched *pernelle street!*
perfected *perrée street!*
petted *petel street!*
petrels in *petrel street!*
presence preserves *de presles street!*

the rents in *de rennes street!*

eh! serpents in *serpente street!*
eh! serene in *serret street!*
eh! severe seven in *seveste street!*

eh! terns in *des ternes street!*
eh! theme: *thérèse street!*

eh! verbs in verderet street!
eh! Verner's in *vernet street!*

weekends in weber *street!*

&
de l'yvette
street!

eh!

It's Been Raining

ru d'aboukir — ru agar — ru d'aix — ru allard — ru alphand
— ru amyot — ru d'anjou — ru d'annam — ru d'antin — ru
d'argout — ru d'arras — ru d'arsonval — ru d'assas — ru auber
— ru aubriot — ru audran — ru aumont — ru d'avron — ru
azaïs —

ru du bac — ru baillou — ru bailly — ru ballu — ru balzac — ru
baron — ru barrault — ru basfroi — ru bassano — ru baudoin
— ru baudricourt — ru baulan — ru bayard — ru bichat — ru
bignon — ru biot — ru bisson— ru bixio — ru bobillot — ru du
boccador — ru boinod — ru borda — ru bosio — ru botha — ru
botzaris — ru bouchardon — ru bouchut — ru boucicaut — ru
boucry — ru bouilloux-laffont — ru boulard — ru boulay — ru
du bouloi — ru bourgon — ru du bourg-tibourg — ru boursault
— ru boussingault — ru boutin — ru brancion — ru broca —
ru brochant — ru bongniart — ru broussais — ru bruant — ru
buffault — ru buffon— — ru du buis — ru bruot — ru burnouf
— ru burq

ru cabanis — ru cadix — ru cail — ru caillaux — ru cambon — ru
campo-formio — ru du canada — ru caplat — ru capron — ru cardan
— ru du cardinal-dubois — ru carucci — ru carolus-duran — ru caron
—ru casablanca — ru cassini — ru catagnary — ru catinat — ru cauchois
— ru cauchy — ru caulaincourt — ru cavalotti —

ru chabanais — ru du chaffault — ru chalgrin — ru chaligny — ru chamfort
— ru champagny — ru champollion — ru chanzy — ru cahpon — ru cahptal — ru

181

chapu — ru chapuis — ru charcot — ru chardin — ru charlot — ru du charolais — ru charras — ru chauchat — ru chaudron — ru choron — ru christiani —

ru cimarosa

. . . .

February,	Rue Soufflot	903 JTJ 75
29/04		48 JWW
"	Rue Clément-Marot	253 JWX
05/05	Rue de Parme	848 JWX
06/05	Opéra	485 JWX
07/05	Rue de Douai	311 JXJ
13/05	Rue de Clichy	688 JXJ
16/05	Trinité	336 JXK
17/05	Franklin-Roosevelt	182 JXM
04/06	Rue Marx-Dormoy	479 JXY
06/06	Saint-Lazare	362 JXZ
"	Rue du Havre	730 JYF
15/06	Rue de Clichy	407 JYX
04/07	?	653 JZC
12/07	?	219 JZF
16/07	Trinité	851 JZG
17/07	Bd. Saint-Martin	754 JZM
19/07	Beaubourg	571 JZP
20/07	Place de l'Europe	867 JZR
10/08	Champs-Élysées	939 JZR
11/08	Gare de Lyon	146 JZW
13/08	Pont Royal	263 KAF
09/08	Rue Lepic	4165 WK 75

The Hour

the hour of awakening of the inhabitants of the passage de la reine de hongrie
the hour of the café opening in rue du moulin de la pointe
the hour of garbage collection in rue du sommet des alpes
the hour of the bakery opening in rue du roi de sicile
the hour of the streetslights going off in the rue du pot de fer
the hour of the butcher opening in rue du faubourg du temple
the hour of the children getting up in rue de la poterne des peupliers
the hour of the delicatessen opening in rue du moulin des prés
the hour of walking the dogs in avenue de la porte de pantin
the hour of cleaning the gutters in rue des nonnains d'hyères
the hour of the garage opening in rue du val de grâce
the hour of airy manners of cats in rue du père teilhard de chardin
the hour of the driving school opening on boulevard des filles du calvaire
the hour of turtledoves cooing in rue du moulin de la vierge
the hour of the hatshop opening in the galerie des marchands de la gare
    saint-lazare
the hour of car invasion in the avenue de la porte d'orléans
the hour of the school opening in avenue de la porte de champerret
the hour of the rumbling of motors in the avenue de la porte d'italie
the hour of the optician opening in rue du pas de la mule
the hour of the mission opening in the rue du pont de lodi
the hour of the libraries opening in rue de l'école de médecine
the hour of the church opening in place d'estienne d'orves
the hour of the brasserie opening in rue du château d'eau
the hour of the electrician opening in rue patrice de la tour du pin
the hour of the salon opening in rue des colonnes du trône
the hour of the flower shop opening in avenue de la porte de montrouge
the hour of the shoemaker opening in rue du dessous des berges
the hour of the jeweler's opening on place de la porte de saint-cloud
the hour of the restaurant opening on avenue de la porte de clichy
the hour of the printer opening in rue de la cour des noues
the hour of the heliport opening on avenue de la porte de sèvres
the hour of the church opening off rue du chevalier de la barre
the hour of the hospital opening in rue de la porte d'aubervilliers
the hour of the funeral home opening on avenue de la porte de clignancourt

the hour of the bath of the sparrows—of the alley of the soleil d'or
the hour of recess for the schoolchildren in rue du val de marne

the hour of asphixiation of pedestrians on avenue de la porte de vitry
the hour of asphixiation of dogs on avenue de la porte de choisy
the hour of asphixiation of cats on avenue de la porte d'ivry
the hour of asphixiation of sparrows on avenue de la porte de gentilly
the hour of asphixiation of children on avenue de la porte de vanves
the hour of asphixiation of lettuce on avenue de la porte de la plaine
the hour of asphixiation of chestnut trees on avenue de la porte d'issy
the hour of asphixiation of drivers on avenue de la porte d'auteuil
the hour of asphixiation of motorcyclists on avenue du parc de passy
the hour of asphixiation of rugbymen on avenue du parc des prices
the hour of asphixiation of bicyclists on avenue de la porte des ternes
the hour of asphixiation of potted violets on avenue de la porte d'asnières
the hour of asphixiation of the geraniums on avenue de la porte de la chapelle
the hour of asphixiation of the lilacs on avenue de la porte des lilas

the hour of lengthening shadows on avenue du maréchal franchet d'espérey
the hour of the chapel closing on avenue de la porte de vincennes
the hour of take-off of pigeons on the place de la porte de versailles
the hour of the café closing in rue du roi d'alger
the hour of lighting the streetlights on the place de la porte de passy
the hour of invisible cats in rue du bois de boulogne
the hour of sleepiness of inhabitants in rue du parc de charonne

the hour of remembering the disappearance of rue du moulin de beurre

185

Hommage to Sébastien Bottin's Telephone Directory

Gérard Dubois	Rue Émile-Dubois
Bruno Petit	Rue Petit
Muriel Legrand	Rue Belgrand
Maurice Leblanc	Rue Louis-Blanc
Martine Marie	Rue Myrrha
Raymond Marie	Rue du Moulin-de-la-Vierge
Chantal Maisonneuve	Rue de l'Exposition
Luc Maisonneuve	Rue des Entrepreneurs
Claudine Rousseau	Boulevard Voltaire

Catherine Baron	Rue Monsieur-le-Prince
Évelyne Baron	Rue Michel-le-Comte
Albert Leroy	Rue des Favorites
Franceline Leroy	Place de la République
Jenny & Jérôme Leroy	Boulevard de Port-Royal
Jean-Luc Dieu	Rue Maison-Dieu
Françoise Dieu	Passage des Soupirs
Thierry Dieu	Rue des Vertus
Maurice Leriche	Rue des Ortolans
François Chevalier	Rue Monsieur-le-Prince
Antoinette Levêque	Rue du Cloître-Notre-Dame
Anne Marie Levêque	Rue de l'Église
Yann Levêque	Rue des Abbesses
Yolande Boulange	Rue René-Boulanger
Gérard Blanc	Rue des Meuniers
Alain Meunier	Rue des Boulangers
Colette Meunier	Rue des Moulins
Frédéric Meunier	Rue du Moulin-Joly
Geneviève Meunier	Rue du Moulin-Vert
Jacques Meunier	Rue du Moulin-des-Prés
Jean Claude Meunier	Rue Jean-Moulin
(and for symmetry)	
Bernard Moulin	Rue des Meuniers
Marguerite Meunier	Rue Moulinet
Pierre Meunier	Rue Stanislas-Meunier

André Dumoulin	Rue du Moulin-Vert
Étienne Couturier	Rue des Petits-Carreaux
Évelybe Renard	Rue des Canettes
Jean-Baptiste Renard	Rue des Anglais
Louise Renard	Rue des Haies
Marcel Leloup	Rue Brèche-aux-Loups
Marc Berger	Rue des Bergers
Didier Fontaine	Rue du Château-d'Eau
François Fontaine	Rue de la Fontaine-au-Roi
Marie Fontaine	Rue La Fontaine
Camille Buisson	Rue des Arbustes
Josie Anne Pin	Rue des Prairies
Caroline Prunier	Rue des Petits-Champs
Agnès Poisson	Quai de l'Oise

Complications

Marinette Boucher	Rue René-Boulanger
Jean Meunier	Rue des Vinaigriers
Pierre Berger	Rue des Meuniers
Marie-Christine Leblond	Boulevard Brune
Amédée Blanc	Boulevard Brune
Daniel Blanc	Boulevard Richard-Lenoir
Marie Blanc	Rue Vertbois
Jacqueline Lenoir	Rue Blance
Carlo Marin	Rue du Mont-Cenis
Christian Marin	Rue du Sahel

They Lived on Rue Campagne-Première in 1983

Jean Marc LECHENE	in number 3
C. BOUQUET	in number 5
Barbara GINGEMBRE	in the same house
Jean-Charles ROSIER	in number 7
Elizabeth QUATREBOEUFS	in number 8b
Marcel FOURMY	in number 12
Lucienne TAUPELET	in the same house
Y. LE. POULAIN	in number 27
C. DESCHAMPS	in number 33

or

Jean Marc OAK	in number 3
C. BOUQUET	in number 5
Barbara GINGER	in the same house
Jean-Charles ROSEBUSH	in number 7
Elizabeth FOURBULLS	in number 8b
Marcel ANT	in number 12
Lucienne MOLE	in the same house
Y. COLT	in number 27
C. FIELDS	in number 33

Songs of Streets and Streets

What the Poet Says in Regard to Flowers,
Fruit, Leaves, and Branches

sad nasturtia
in Paris inertia

sad cherries
Paris harries

sad sad figs
Paris frigs

sad the thickets
given parking tickets

sad sad phlox
that Paris mocks

sad the willows
bent in billows

sad violets
Paris forgets

sad holly oaks
that Paris chokes

sad cherry (wild kind)
in Paris? out of your mind!

197

sad mimosa
in Paris half froza

sad morning glories
run over by lorries

sad wistaria
in Paris hysteria

sad bindweeds
Paris bleeds

sad daffodils
in Paris no pleasure fills

sad peppermint
that Paris will stint

sad the gardenia
in Paris schizophrenia

sad sad aster
Paris spells disaster

sad cammelia
with Garbophilia

sas sad hedge
where Paris drives a wedge

sad boxwood too
nothing in Paris for you

sad sad jasmine
in Paris you're a has-been

sad thistle
Paris has blown your whistle

sad sad vines
Paris undermines

sad pimpernels
Paris quells

sad sad pear
you'll die in Paris air

sad tulips
that Paris wind whips

sad sad roses
of which Paris disposes

sad tree the plane
in Paris slain

sad olive grove
that Paris overdrove

sad cypress sad
from being had

sad sad field
walled and sealed

sad lilac
a lot like my luck

sad iris
in Paris tires us

sad sad elms
Paris overwhelms

sad lily
Paris finds silly

sad prairies
Paris buries

sad the shrubs
Paris snubs

sad licorice
in Paris piss

sad fern
for Paris to burn

sad rushes
Paris crushes

sad sad mint
for Paris to stint

sad crocus
in Paris lack focus

sad cowslips
the Paris frost nips

sad sycamores
Paris ignores

sad mountain ash
in Paris you'll crash

sad turmeric
Paris turns you sick

so sad

Place du Général-Brocard
1885-1950
Member of the National Assembly

He's got his place
To preserve his trace
But no boulevard
For General Brocard

Park Monceau's gate
In fine gilded state
Shows high regard
For General Brocard

The National Assembly
Received all meek and trembly
(A filibuster bard?)
General Brocard

Through Rue de Courcelles
Cars rush pell-mell
But blithely disregard
General Brocard

True, Avenue Hoche
Could serve as an approach
But relegates to backyard
Place du General Brocard

Still, it's a short space
From Étoile to the place

That remains the calling card
Of General Brocard

Ouf!

Ah!

Ah! what silence
In Rue de Valence!
But what alarm
In Rue de Parme!

Calm ah! how calm
In Rue des Palmes
Such agitation on
Rue Brancion

Ah! how serene
Is the Rue de Seine!
But what disquietude
Boulevard de Dixmude!

Ah! trouble stem to stern
Along Avenue de Ternes
For ultimate rest
Rue Gît-le-Coeur's still best.

Ah!

Song of Rue Custine
and Rue Caulaincourt

He hawked sardines
And guided a tour
Twixt Rue Custine
And Rue Caulaincourt

She baked Boston beans
And boiled confiture
Twixt Rue Custine
And Rue Caulaincourt

She was oh so clean
Her skin so pure
Twixt Rue Custine
And Rue Caulaincourt

Such a girl he'd never seen
Blood pressure cut short his tour
Twixt Rue Custine
And Rue Caulaincourt

She played the queen
He proved a boor
Twixt Rue Custine
And Rue Caulaincourt

She struck out for a distant beach
With a dealer in drink-and-victual
Leaving within his reach
Damn little:

Her beans his sardines
And his abbreviated tour
Twixt Rue Custine
And Rue Caulaincourt

Rues Madame and Monsieur

He walked one day on Rue Madame
One day she walked on Rue Monsieur
Rue Madame is laid with macadam
True no less for Rue Monsieur.

Gladly he strolled down Rue Madame
Calmly she ambled Rue Monsieur
A day without drama on Rue Madame
Delightful day on Rue Monsieur.

You can see the sky from Rue Madame
From Rue Monsieur the skies unfold
All cats are gray in Rue Madame
In Rue Monsieur all cats are old.

She never went down Rue Madame
He never went up Rue Monsieur
Never their eyes met flame with flame
Never a vow from either breast

And maybe that's all for the best.

He walked away by Rue Madame
She walked away by Rue Monsieur
Rue Madame is laid with macadam
True no less for Rue Monsieur.

Storm at Nine

You slog through mud without a buoy
On Place Félix-Éboué

From flower pots with strainer holes
Down Rue du Ruisseau a steady trickle rolls

Waters backed up in a feverish furl
Bisect Rue de Bièvre's swirl

Waterdrop, waterdrip, drop encore
in Passage de la Goutte-d'Or

Drowned to the scuttle of your boot
Rue Noyer-Durand, Boulevard Soult!

Sour floods on Rue de la Sourdière
In Rue La Fontaine, sinkholes everywhere

Marshland or pond, no moorings mar
Rue Mariotte and Rue de la Mare

Moisture froths moss into mousse
Rue de Moussy, Impasse Mousset

Passage des Orgues, the organs grind
Out hurricanes, this wind wind wind.

When

When will the wind have taken all of you
Water washed your every image away
Emptied out fold by fold of my brain
The camphor reek of your death day

When will my tongue attacking you
Grown pallid, finish its attack
Your scape completely stripped
Of sky's blue and of dirt's black

When will ceasing cease, cease
From unceasing pressure, the press
Of your cold eye across my rods and cones

When will earth, the earth between
Bark and sap, assume the weight
Of your sedentary bones

Rue d'Amsterdam

Rue d'Amsterdam goes down goes up
Goes up and down it does, my street
I go up or go down Rue d'Amsterdam
Go down go up my Amsterdam Street

We say we go up say we go down
Streets that go up and streets going down
Say it even of hesitant streets
Or streets on absolutely level ground

We go up streets on the macadam
Walk on the sidewalk down the street
So I go down my Rue d'Amsterdam
So I climb my Amsterdam Street

What is it goes down and what goes up
Goes down or not in every street?
Is it the houses that go up and up
Or falling fall toward the bottom of the street?

It's the houses, they go by number
The one on the door that faces the street
If the street goes down so do the numbers
And if the numbers go up so does the street

But why do we say that numbers go up
Climbing from naught to infinite height?
Because numbers form a street of numbers
The street of whole numbers outdistancing night

Long indeed the high road of numbers
The high abstract road, no end to that way
You go up you go down you count and recount
The world-long night where all numbers are gray

But maybe our streets are just shadows
Shadows of numbers that fall in the rain
Remnants and ends of the street of numbers
Going up going down while our lives remain

Quiet Days at Porte d'Orléans

Quiet Days at Porte d'Orléans

for Pierre Lusson

Avenue Ernest-Reyer
is nearly in the south
subs
you cross the bridge over the perif
and there you are

The house is sort of empty
Matthew has gone to Montrouge (with Yuka)
Cecile has gone to Villejuif (with Philippe (and Ferdinand))
Juliette has gone to Montreal (Quebec) (with Patrick)
They've gone
it's calm!
not just
"when dawn discretely
reddens in a pure sky"
but even
at that "quiet hour when the li-ons drink?
i. e., generally
nightfall

There's plenty of room for ruckus
& for the "Mac"
& for the printer
& for the kitchen chores
& for the office chores
with all the files, all the books
keeping an eye on Theory

and its supposed
developments

Retirement

Outside leaves
are falling

(1991)

An Address to the Streets of Paris

"Rue—
Madame,
Mademoiselle,
Monsieur"

etc.

Paris

awakens
belongs to us
is cold, is hungry, no longer eats chestnuts on the street,
etc.

Of Paris

the peasant
the pedestrian
the crossing
the troubles
the mysteries
the ruins
the Mohicans
the fall
the belly

the meridian

of Paris

Pont Mirabeau

"Under pont Mirabeau flows the Seine"
"Why bring it up so often then?"

Pont Mirabeau

Under Pont Mirabeau flows the Yonne[1]
And our loves
So do I have to keep in monne
How joy comes always after ponne.

---

[1] When two currents of water differently named[2] come together, the river that results from their confluence takes the name of the one whose level is higher at the point where they meet. According to the most recent calculations, the river in Paris called Seine should be called the Yonne.

[2] If they have the same name (which happens rarely), they keep it.

Rue des Entrepreneurs

—Where do you live?
—Rue du Loing.
—That's not close.
—And you?
—Rue du Clos.
—That's a long ways.

Hotel des Deux Acacias

The Hotel des Deux Acacias
Displays two stars
Were it "des Trois Acacias"
Would it have three?

Quiet Days at Porte d'Orléans, 2

for Pierre Lusson

Avenue Ernest-Reyer
is nearly in the south
subs
you cross the bridge over the perif
and there you are

The house is sort of empty
Matthew has gone to Montrouge (with Yuka) (and Izumi)
Cecile has gone to Villejuif (with Philippe (and Ferdinand) (and
    Capucine))
Juliette has gone to Montreal (Quebec)
They've gone
it's calm!
not just
"when dawn discretely
reddens in a pure sky"
but even
at that "quiet hour when the li-ons drink"
i.e., generally
nightfall

There's plenty of room for ruckus
& for the "Mac"
& for the printer
& for the kitchen chores
& for the office chores
with all the files, all the books

224

keeping an eye on Theory
and its supposed
developments

Retirement

Outside leaves
are falling

(1993)

Rome's No Longer in Rome, etc.

> *Paris, which is only Paris*
> *while ripping up its paving stones*
> Aragon 1944?

"Its paving stones"?

Like where?

Piratewatch 1996
(Gare Saint-Lazare, by loudspeaker)

"Travelers are requested not to leave children or aged relatives unattended; they are liable to be destroyed by security."

Rue Pavée

Rue Pavée

is no longer paved.

De

no one says "Place de Clichy"
no one says "Rue Clichy"

Square

square, skwair, skerry, scary, scare, squared,
squary, squat, scat, scarlet, secret, sea crest,
seek rest, skelp, skelter, skepsis, skerry, sherry,
sketch, skew, skibob, skidoo, scarab, score,
screech, scream, screw, skitter, skid, skull,
skulk, skullduggery, saccharine, scribble, squire, squirrel.

Passage Choiseul

August 15, the Passage Choiseul is closed
The eye is out of choices

Rue Vieille-du-Temple,
1983

Constriction. disarmed. extravagantly
Heavy.
Left to vague
Disasters,
By a blood-sentence
Unmoored,

Beating heart
Container without content. without.
Today's summary:
Nothing
Or nothing.
Tomorrow: same.

Will be what will be
Her colors:
White, White
The sun, the sun, the sun
White
Meanwhile empties

Your words pierced
Your thought shunned
Words
That don't words
Cries hidden, hidden, becoming inured
To the worst

Refusal:
Eye, and breast, finger
Cold weight that your hand's doing its best
Insane, inconsistent
To bend.
In order to.

Air,
Commotion,
Against the angle
Of this blue
Rue Vieille-du-Temple
Wrong way. go 'way. no safeguard.

Alone, Rue Sainte-Anne,
the Monday of Pentecost 1995

Anne, Rue Sainte-Anne, I see nothing coming!

Quiet Days at Porte d'Orléans, 3
(1995 version)

for Pierre Lusson

Avenue Ernest-Reyer
is nearly in the south
subs
you cross the bridge over the perif
and there you are

The house is sort of empty
Matthew has gone to Montrouge (with Yuka) (and Izumi)
Cecile has gone to Villejuif (with Philippe (and Ferdinand) (and
    Capucine) (and Angèle))
Juliette has gone to Montreal (Quebec)
They've gone
it's calm!
not just
"when dawn discretely
reddens in a pure sky"
but even
at that "quiet hour when the li-ons drink"
i.e., generally
nightfall

There's plenty of room for ruckus
& for the "Mac"
& for the printer
& for the kitchen chores
& for the office chores

with all the files, all the books
keeping an eye on Theory
and its supposed
developments

Retirement

Outside leaves
are falling

Undated Night, Rue Saint-Jacques

Among a Lot of Poems

Among a lot of poems
There was one
I could never quite bring to mind
Except that I had composed it
A while back
Going down this street
This street on the even-numbered side
Bathed in a morning light
A street of small persistent shops
Between the stricken Seine and the hospital
A poem I wrote with my feet
As I compose all my poems
Silently in my head walking
But I remember nothing
Except the street the light and the chance
That had put into this poem
The word "respect"
A word I wouldn't ordinarily set pulsing
Across my mind's pages of poetry
Beyond that nothing
And this word this word that won't budge
Witnesses the end of that street
Like a tree space has forgotten

Undated Night, Rue Saint-Jacques

The street grave, black, black, the black street black grave there.

The street grave, black, black, the black grave, black street, there.

The street grave, black, black; grave, the black street black, there.

The street, black black grave, black street, the black grave, there.

The street grave, black; black black street, there, black grave, there.

The street grave, black, the black black street, grave black there.

The street grave, black, the black, black, black street, grave there.

The street grave, black, black there; black grave, black street there.

The street, grave, there. Black, black grave, black street, black there.

The street grave, black; black, the black black street-grave; there.

The street grave. The black street black. Black grave black. There.

Translators' Notes

p. 5   *after Raymond Queneau*: this poem, and many of the poems to follow in this section, are direct "replies" to specific poems in Queneau's book *Courir les rues* [Running the Streets]. "Paris" refers to the first stanza of his *"L'Amphion."*

p. 6   a Verlaine quatrain: Roubaud is pointing out that the alternating lines of seven and eight syllables make "Paris," the preceding poem, a rather typical Verlainian quatrain. Queneau had done the same with a sign in a public restroom in his poem *"Les pauvres gens."*

p. 9   No more "little old shop": see Queneau's "Rue Volta."

p. 12   Hell or Heaven: *Le Ciel* and *l'Enfer* were twin cafes on Boulevard de Clichy until 1954. *Le Néant*, another café, still existed in 1967 when Queneau wrote his poem "Boulevard de Clichy," lamenting the disappearance of Heaven and Hell but taking comfort in the fact that there was still Nothing.

p. 13   Square Marigny: in Queneau's poem *"Ce jour-là,"* he reports having bought a Marcel Proust stamp at the square.

p. 15   not only at Lilas: a reference to Serge Gainsbourg's song, *"Le poinçonneur des Lilas."*

p. 15   *Sold anvils "on the run"*: the French humorist Pierre Dac had a sketch in which he enumerated all the trades he had plied, each more absurd than the next. It's one thing to have a business "on the run" in the Métro (where hawking is illegal)—but with anvils?

p. 18 *Les mères de famille*: "The mothers of [*mères de*] a family tell you shit [*merde*] on families."

p. 18 *La morale de cette histoir'là*: "The moral of this story, ah / story, ah: / girls that've got no papa / got no papa / should not be sent to school in Batignolles."

p. 18 Mur des Fédérés: the wall in Père Lachaise cemetery where the revolutionaries of the Paris Commune of 1870 were executed.

p. 35 "in a few round smoke rings"/ "that perish in further rings": see Mallarmé's *"Toute l'âme résumée . . ."* in *Plusieurs Sonnets.*

p. 37 *Pont des Arts*: see Apollinaire's *"Le Pont Mirabeau"* and singer/songwriter George Brassens's *"Le Vent."*

p. 39 *A Poem for Claude Roy*: cf. Apollinaire's *"Le Chat"* (in *"Le Bestiaire"*) and *"L'adieu."*

p. 47 "the end, harbor, daybreak": a line by Étienne Jodelle (1532-1573), poet and dramatist, member of the Pléiade.

p. 58 who could not count to twenty: as pointed out by Jacques Prévert in his poem *"Les belles familles."*

p. 59 Montagne: during the French Revolution, "Montagne" was the name given to the group of members of the National Convention who occupied the highest benches and always voted for the most violent measures.

p. 61   "The black-currant river . . ." / "The shadows of trees . . .":
         see Rimbaud's *"La rivière de cassis"* and Verlaine's *"Romances
         sans paroles IX."*

p. 68   *"Autumn in the air"*: play on *Winter in the Air*, a collection of
         stories by Sylvia Townsend Warner.

p. 69   Tsaritsyne: ancient name of Stalingrad.

p. 70   Charles Martel: "The Hammer," 688-741, Frankish ruler,
         natural son of Pippin II and grandfather of Charlemagne.
         His decisive victory at Poitiers (732) stopped the Arabic
         expansion from Spain northward. He also conquered Frisia
         and Alemannia.

p. 73   K-way: a brand of raincoat.

p. 93   quite unquiet hamlets: cf. Baudelaire's *"La Géante."*

p. 133   Joseph Hall (1574-1656) is remembered (rather dimly) for his
         satires—and for his unjustified claim to be the first English
         satirist. He also wrote a number of devotional works, includ-
         ing *The Art of Divine Meditation* (1607), containing, as appen-
         dix, "A Meditation of Death, according to the former Rules."
         Roubaud uses only the rubrics of this exemplary meditation,
         accepting its subject but not its presuppositions, and writes a
         sonnet for each heading (Hall's meditation is in prose).

p. 160   *Invitation to a Voyage*: cf. Baudelaire's *"L'Invitation au voy-
         age."*

p. 168   *The Trade in Classics*: the French reader would recognize
         the mnemonic sentence to help remember the names of the

principal classics: "*Une* corneille *perchée sur une* racine *de* bruyère, *boit l'eau de* la fontaine molière," literally, a crow perched on a briar root drinks the water of the millstone fountain.

p. 170   "elementary morality": the shape of these three poems is modeled on the first section of Queneau's *Morale élémentaire*.

p. 181   *It's Been Raining*: The *rue*s have turned into *ru*s, gullies, due to the French title of this poem, *Il a plu*.

p. 183   *Licence Portrait of Paris 1992*: The column on the right represents Paris license plates whose numbers are followed by letters (now usually three). Their chronology is encoded alphabetically. In the course of the poem one gets from J to K. The last car mentioned is very old because its plaque has only two letters.

p. 195   *Songs of Streets and Streets*: a reference to Victor Hugo's *Les chansons des rues et des bois*.

p. 197   *What the Poet Says in Regard to Flowers, Fruit, Leaves, and Branches*: cf. Rimbaud's poem "*Ce qu'on dit au poète à propos de fleurs*" [What One Says to the Poet in Regard to Flowers].

p. 218   *Paris*: Olivier Assayas: *Paris Awakens*
Jacques Rivette: *Paris Belongs to Us*
The last two lines quote from Paul Eluard's "*Courage*" (1942).

p. 219   Includes titles by Aragon, Léon-Paul Fargue, Marcel Aymé,

Boileau, Eugène Sue, Jacques Réda, Ilya Ehrenbourg, Emile Zola, and Jacques Réda.

p. 227   *Piratewatch*: *Vigipirate* is the name of the antiterrorist measures meant to accustom the French to the presence of armed soldiers and police in the streets, the French version of "Homeland Security."

Jacques Roubaud is the author of numerous books, including the novels *The Great Fire of London* and *The Loop*, and the poetry collection *Some Thing Black*. He is one of the most accomplished members of the Oulipo.

FOR A FULL LIST OF PUBLICATIONS, VISIT:
www.dalkeyarchive.com

MAX FRISCH, *I'm Not Stiller.*
Man in the Holocene.
CARLOS FUENTES, *Christopher Unborn.*
Distant Relations.
Terra Nostra.
Where the Air Is Clear.
JANICE GALLOWAY, *Foreign Parts.*
The Trick Is to Keep Breathing.
WILLIAM H. GASS, *Cartesian Sonata and Other Novellas.*
Finding a Form.
A Temple of Texts.
The Tunnel.
Willie Masters' Lonesome Wife.
GÉRARD GAVARRY, *Hoppla! 1 2 3.*
ETIENNE GILSON,
The Arts of the Beautiful.
Forms and Substances in the Arts.
C. S. GISCOMBE, *Giscome Road.*
Here.
Prairie Style.
DOUGLAS GLOVER, *Bad News of the Heart.*
The Enamoured Knight.
WITOLD GOMBROWICZ,
A Kind of Testament.
KAREN ELIZABETH GORDON,
The Red Shoes.
GEORGI GOSPODINOV, *Natural Novel.*
JUAN GOYTISOLO, *Count Julian.*
Juan the Landless.
Makbara.
Marks of Identity.
PATRICK GRAINVILLE, *The Cave of Heaven.*
HENRY GREEN, *Back.*
Blindness.
Concluding.
Doting.
Nothing.
JIŘÍ GRUŠA, *The Questionnaire.*
GABRIEL GUDDING,
Rhode Island Notebook.
MELA HARTWIG, *Am I a Redundant Human Being?*
JOHN HAWKES, *The Passion Artist.*
Whistlejacket.
ALEKSANDAR HEMON, ED.,
Best European Fiction.
AIDAN HIGGINS, *A Bestiary.*
Balcony of Europe.
Bornholm Night-Ferry.
Darkling Plain: Texts for the Air.
Flotsam and Jetsam.
Langrishe, Go Down.
Scenes from a Receding Past.
Windy Arbours.
KEIZO HINO, *Isle of Dreams.*
ALDOUS HUXLEY, *Antic Hay.*
Crome Yellow.
Point Counter Point.
Those Barren Leaves.
Time Must Have a Stop.
MIKHAIL IOSSEL AND JEFF PARKER, EDS.,
Amerika: Russian Writers View the United States.
GERT JONKE, *The Distant Sound.*
Geometric Regional Novel.

Homage to Czerny.
The System of Vienna.
JACQUES JOUET, *Mountain R.*
Savage.
CHARLES JULIET, *Conversations with Samuel Beckett and Bram van Velde.*
MIEKO KANAI, *The Word Book.*
YORAM KANIUK, *Life on Sandpaper.*
HUGH KENNER, *The Counterfeiters.*
Flaubert, Joyce and Beckett: The Stoic Comedians.
Joyce's Voices.
DANILO KIŠ, *Garden, Ashes.*
A Tomb for Boris Davidovich.
ANITA KONKKA, *A Fool's Paradise.*
GEORGE KONRÁD, *The City Builder.*
TADEUSZ KONWICKI, *A Minor Apocalypse.*
The Polish Complex.
MENIS KOUMANDAREAS, *Koula.*
ELAINE KRAF, *The Princess of 72nd Street.*
JIM KRUSOE, *Iceland.*
EWA KURYLUK, *Century 21.*
EMILIO LASCANO TEGUI, *On Elegance While Sleeping.*
ERIC LAURRENT, *Do Not Touch.*
VIOLETTE LEDUC, *La Bâtarde.*
SUZANNE JILL LEVINE, *The Subversive Scribe: Translating Latin American Fiction.*
DEBORAH LEVY, *Billy and Girl.*
Pillow Talk in Europe and Other Places.
JOSÉ LEZAMA LIMA, *Paradiso.*
ROSA LIKSOM, *Dark Paradise.*
OSMAN LINS, *Avalovara.*
The Queen of the Prisons of Greece.
ALF MAC LOCHLAINN,
The Corpus in the Library.
Out of Focus.
RON LOEWINSOHN, *Magnetic Field(s).*
BRIAN LYNCH, *The Winner of Sorrow.*
D. KEITH MANO, *Take Five.*
MICHELINE AHARONIAN MARCOM,
The Mirror in the Well.
BEN MARCUS,
The Age of Wire and String.
WALLACE MARKFIELD,
Teitlebaum's Window.
To an Early Grave.
DAVID MARKSON, *Reader's Block.*
Springer's Progress.
Wittgenstein's Mistress.
CAROLE MASO, *AVA.*
LADISLAV MATEJKA AND KRYSTYNA POMORSKA, EDS.,
Readings in Russian Poetics: Formalist and Structuralist Views.
HARRY MATHEWS,
The Case of the Persevering Maltese: Collected Essays.
Cigarettes.
The Conversions.
The Human Country: New and Collected Stories.
The Journalist.

CHRISTINE SCHUTT, *Nightwork.*
GAIL SCOTT, *My Paris.*
DAMION SEARLS, *What We Were Doing*
and Where We Were Going.
JUNE AKERS SEESE,
Is This What Other Women Feel Too?
What Waiting Really Means.
BERNARD SHARE, *Inish.*
Transit.
AURELIE SHEEHAN,
Jack Kerouac Is Pregnant.
VIKTOR SHKLOVSKY, *Knight's Move.*
A Sentimental Journey:
Memoirs 1917–1922.
Energy of Delusion: A Book on Plot.
Literature and Cinematography.
Theory of Prose.
Third Factory.
Zoo, or Letters Not about Love.
CLAUDE SIMON, *The Invitation.*
PIERRE SINIAC, *The Collaborators.*
JOSEF ŠKVORECKÝ, *The Engineer of*
Human Souls.
GILBERT SORRENTINO,
Aberration of Starlight.
Blue Pastoral.
Crystal Vision.
Imaginative Qualities of Actual
Things.
Mulligan Stew.
Pack of Lies.
Red the Fiend.
The Sky Changes.
Something Said.
Splendide-Hôtel.
Steelwork.
Under the Shadow.
W. M. SPACKMAN,
The Complete Fiction.
ANDRZEJ STASIUK, *Fado.*
GERTRUDE STEIN,
Lucy Church Amiably.
The Making of Americans.
A Novel of Thank You.
LARS SVENDSEN, *A Philosophy of Evil.*
PIOTR SZEWC, *Annihilation.*
GONÇALO M. TAVARES, *Jerusalem.*
LUCIAN DAN TEODOROVICI,
Our Circus Presents . . .
STEFAN THEMERSON, *Hobson's Island.*
The Mystery of the Sardine.
Tom Harris.
JOHN TOOMEY, *Sleepwalker.*
JEAN-PHILIPPE TOUSSAINT,
The Bathroom.
Camera.
Monsieur.
Running Away.
Self-Portrait Abroad.
Television.
DUMITRU TSEPENEAG,
Hotel Europa.
The Necessary Marriage.
Pigeon Post.
Vain Art of the Fugue.
ESTHER TUSQUETS, *Stranded.*

DUBRAVKA UGRESIC,
Lend Me Your Character.
Thank You for Not Reading.
MATI UNT, *Brecht at Night.*
Diary of a Blood Donor.
Things in the Night.
ÁLVARO URIBE AND OLIVIA SEARS, EDS.,
Best of Contemporary Mexican
Fiction.
ELOY URROZ, *Friction.*
The Obstacles.
LUISA VALENZUELA, *He Who Searches.*
MARJA-LIISA VARTIO,
The Parson's Widow.
PAUL VERHAEGHEN, *Omega Minor.*
BORIS VIAN, *Heartsnatcher.*
LLORENÇ VILLALONGA, *The Dolls' Room.*
ORNELA VORPSI, *The Country Where No*
One Ever Dies.
AUSTRYN WAINHOUSE, *Hedyphagetica.*
PAUL WEST,
Words for a Deaf Daughter & Gala.
CURTIS WHITE,
America's Magic Mountain.
The Idea of Home.
Memories of My Father Watching TV.
Monstrous Possibility: An Invitation
to Literary Politics.
Requiem.
DIANE WILLIAMS, *Excitability:*
Selected Stories.
Romancer Erector.
DOUGLAS WOOLF, *Wall to Wall.*
Ya! & John-Juan.
JAY WRIGHT, *Polynomials and Pollen.*
The Presentable Art of Reading
Absence.
PHILIP WYLIE, *Generation of Vipers.*
MARGUERITE YOUNG,
Angel in the Forest.
Miss MacIntosh, My Darling.
REYOUNG, *Unbabbling.*
VLADO ŽABOT, *The Succubus.*
ZORAN ŽIVKOVIĆ, *Hidden Camera.*
LOUIS ZUKOFSKY, *Collected Fiction.*
SCOTT ZWIREN, *God Head.*